MUSEUM OF FINE ARTS BUDAPEST

Newsweek / GREAT MUSEUMS OF THE WORLD

NEW YORK, N.Y.

**GREAT MUSEUMS
OF THE WORLD**

Editorial Director:
Henry A. La Farge

MUSEUM OF FINE ARTS BUDAPEST

Introduction by:
Klára Garas

Commentary texts by:
Luc Menaše

Design by:
Gradimir Avramov

Published by:

NEWSWEEK, INC.
& ARNOLDO MONDADORI EDITORE

ISBN 0-88225-315-8

Library of Congress 81-86488

© 1982 — Arnoldo Mondadori Editore — CEAM — Milan

All rights reserved. Printed and bound in Italy
by Arnoldo Mondadori, Verona

INTRODUCTION

Klára Garas
Director, Budapest Museum of Fine Arts

The Budapest Museum of Fine Arts has long been recognized as one of the outstanding museums in Europe. Though not the largest, it is of primary importance by reason of the diversity and historical continuity of its holdings, and particularly because of the high proportion of major works in its keeping. Long well known to scholars and connoisseurs, either through personal experience or art publications, the Museum in recent years has become the focus of widening public attention, as a result of the increased ease of travel and improved communications.

Unlike so many European art museums, the Budapest Museum did not originate as a royal collection. Its foundation is associated with a national revival. Of comparatively recent date in its present form—it first opened its doors to the general public in 1906—the works of art in its possession look back upon two centuries of collecting and cultural aspirations. It owes its existence to the assimilation of several art collections and galleries joined together as a national collection. In time new acquisitions were made and the areas represented were considerably expanded. For many years the collection included Hungarian art as well as that of other countries, but the numerous additions in all fields made it necessary to find a new solution. It was decided to separate the works of Hungarian artists and place them in another museum. In 1957 the Hungarian National Gallery came into being and was installed in the newly renovated Buda castle, thereby assembling a comprehensive representation of purely Hungarian art. As a result, since 1974 the Museum of Fine Arts has been devoted exclusively to works by artists from all other countries.

The history of these collections goes back a long time, and the formation of the galleries reflects the situation of Hungary through the ages. During the wars of the 16th and 17th centuries the art treasures of the Hungarian kings were for the most part lost or destroyed. The famous collection belonging to King Matthias Corvinus, which was kept in the royal castle of Buda and included magnificent illuminated manuscripts, along with Renaissance paintings and sculptures received as gifts from Italian rulers, were dispersed after the king's death; a Madonna by Leonardo da Vinci, which Lodovico Sforza gave to Corvinus, and a bas-relief by Verrocchio, are known to have been among these treasures.

The Turkish conquest, the fall of Buda, and the subsequent division of the state into three parts interrupted the conservation and collecting of art for more than a century. The seat of rule under the Habsburg emperor, who was simultaneously king of Hungary, was in Vienna and Prague. Consequently the imperial collections were formed in those cities and a great many of Hungary's art treasures were transferred there. After a hundred and fifty years of war, it was not until the end of the Turkish occupation and the liberation of the country in the 18th century that a revival of the arts and systematic collecting was again possible.

The first Hungarian collection was initiated in 1802 by Count Ferenc Széchényi with the creation of the National Museum. Between 1832 and 1836 were added the collections of Miklós Janković and of János László Pyrker, Archbishop of Eger. New acquisitions accrued to the National Museum during the Hungarian revolution of 1848, and in the 1860s the Museum acquired an exceptionally valuable collection from the Esterházy family, from whom the Hungarian government purchased 635 pictures. In 1871 the State Gallery was established, and this became the embryo of the present great Museum of Fine Arts. The next year the State Gallery received the fine collection of Bishop Arnold Ipolyi and this was followed by many other important purchases. This created a serious problem of space, so that in 1896 the National Assembly decided to construct a new museum at government expense. The vast building was completed in ten years and was opened to the public in 1906 as the Museum of Fine Arts. In 1912 the Museum received the legacy of Count János Pálffy, but the First World War and the postwar period checked further expansion. During the Second World War, the institution suffered great damage and its most important works were hastily shipped to Germany; but after the war the splendid collection owned by György Ráth was acquired, along with several other collections and the treasures returned by Germany. The Museum has also acquired many works from other museums in Hungary where they had previously been kept, a policy which has been continued.

With holdings of over one hundred thousand objects, the Budapest Museum today offers a comprehensive survey of human creative achievements in art from ancient times to the present day. Most of the works, arranged in chronological order, are on permanent display. The vast ground-floor hall houses the Egyptian collection—newly installed in 1972—and, in keeping with reconstruction plans, a part of the ancient Greek and Roman collections, a fine selection of Italian frescoes and fountains, 19th-century sculpture, and space for the exhibition of contemporary art. Also situated on the ground floor is the graphic arts hall, where exhibitions of prints and Hungarian art are organized either as one-man shows or based on some theme, and occasionally the work of foreign artists.

10   On the first floor is situated the so-called Gallery of Old Masters, containing 600 of the

Museum's best known and most valuable paintings. As the outstanding works of some 2,000 paintings in the possession of the Museum, they are kept on permanent display, and the balance kept in storage, accessible for study or drawn on for occasional exhibitions.

These masterpieces, exhibited chronologically and according to country of origin and school, serve to illustrate the development of Western European painting from the Italian Trecento to the 19th century, with notable works for each period and trend. The Italian section begins with 13th-century Tuscan art, followed by 14th-and 15th-century Florentine and Sienese altarpieces. First-rate works by Aretino Spinello, Sassetta, Domenico Ghirlandajo, and Francesco Francia, offer a comprehensive view of the development of the late Gothic and early Renaissance painting. This is followed by a whole range of masterpieces from the Italian Renaissance: Giorgione's *Portrait of a Young Man*, Raphael's *Portrait of a Young Humanist* and his *Virgin and Child and St. John the Baptist*, a Leonardesque *Virgin and Child* by Boltraffio, Correggio's famous *Madonna del Latte*, Jacopo Bassano's dramatic *Christ Bearing the Cross*, Sebastiano del Piombo's *Portrait of a Man*, and canvases by Titian, Tintoretto, Veronese. The Italian Mannerist and Baroque styles are also represented by major artists— Angelo Bronzino, Annibale Carracci, Guido Reni, Guercino, Bernardo Strozzi and others— while from the 18th-century art are impressive works by G.B. Tiepolo, Sebastiano Ricci, Bernardo Bellotto and the Guardi brothers.

A visitor to the Budapest Museum can also obtain a comprehensive idea of the development of Flemish and Dutch painting. Noteworthy among the 15th-century works are the *Virgin and Child* panel painting by Jan van Eyck's disciple, Petrus Christus, an expressive *Adoration of the Shepherds* by Gerard David, a *Triptych of the Crucifixion* by Hans Memling: and outstanding among the 16th-century paintings are Pieter Brueghel's *Sermon of St. John the Baptist*, Barend van Orley's *Portrait of Charles V*, and Pieter Aertsen's *Market Scene*. Notable examples from the early 17th century are Rubens' and van Dyck's powerful collaborative historical painting, *Mucius Scaevola in the Presence of Porsenna*, Rubens' *Study of a Head*, and two paintings by van Dyck, one from his early period and *Portrait of a Couple* from his later period; there are also a number of important works by Jacob Jordaens along with landscapes and still-lifes of the period. Dutch art of the 17th century is seen in a number of exceptional works. In addition to two male portraits by Frans Hals one can see Rembrandt's *Dream of St. Joseph,* his *Old Rabbi,* and his *Slaughtered Ox,* as well as the joint work of Rembrandt and Gerard Dou, *Hidden Treasure.* There is also a large selection of paintings by the artists who followed in the footsteps of Rembrandt, including Nicolaes Maes, Aert de Gelder and Gerbrandt van den Eeckout. Other outstanding Dutch artists permanently on view are Salomon and Jacob van Ruisdael, Jan van Goyen, and Albert Cuyp. Examples of the work of Vermeer van Delft, the genre painter Adriaen van Ostade, the still-life painter Jan van Huysum also attest to the variety of trends and subject matter presented by the Museum. But altogether these represent only a fraction of the landscapes, still-lifes, portraits and other Netherlandish paintings in the Museum's collections.

The somewhat more limited representation of French painting includes a variety of 17-century works by Nicolas Poussin, Claude Lorrain, Simon Vouet, Pierre Mignard, Nicolas de Largillière, while the 18th century is restricted to canvases by Chardin, Hubert Robert, Greuze, and Boilly.

On the other hand, the Museum possesses an unusually large collection of German and Austrian paintings ranging from the 15th to the late 18th century, and illustrating all the major schools and trends. Especially worthy of notice is the early 15th-century *Death of the Virgin* by Hans Holbein the Elder. The German Renaissance selection is outstandingly represented with works by Albrecht Dürer, Hans Baldung Grien, Albrecht Altdorfer, and Lucas Cranach the Elder, although one should also mention examples by Johann Heinrich Schönefeld and Christoph Pandiss—17th-century German artists whose works are not often seen. From the 18th century are altarpieces, designs for ceiling decorations, portraits, and landscapes by Jan Kupecký, Daniel Oran, Franz Anton Maulbertsch, Angelica Kauffmann, and A. Raphael Mengs.

Because English painting can be found in very few countries outside of Britain, the Budapest collection is worthy of special notice. Some fine examples by Reynolds, Raeburn, Gainsborough, and Lawrence show the development of English portrait painting as it reached its culmination in the 18th century; and for the 19th century, attractive Constable landscapes should be noted.

The portion of the Old Masters Gallery which is best known outside Hungary is the Spanish collection. The seventy paintings in the Budapest Museum constitute an exceptional record of the development of Spanish painting. There are seven paintings by the Greek-born El Greco, among which are the early *Repentant Magdalen*, the mystical late *Agony in the Garden*, and the superbly visionary *Annunciation*. The art of Jusepe de Ribera, who worked in Naples, is seen in his monumental *Martyrdom of St. Andrew*; Velázquez in his early *Company at Table*; and Murillo and Zurbarán each in three outstanding works. Goya's *Water-Carrier, Knife-Grinder* and the *Portrait of Señora Bermúdes* are among the best known and frequently cited of his paintings. In addition to the greatest masters the visitor will come across a number of lesser known artists who are nevertheless significant in the development of Spanish painting, such as Louis Tristan, Francisco de Herrera, Escalante, Alonso Cano, Juan Batisto des Mazo, Carreño de Miranda, and Antonio Pereda.

As a sequel to the Gallery of Old Masters, the so-called Modern Gallery presents an overall view of 19th- and 20th-century painting. There is a rich and varied selection of works associated with Austrian Biedermeier, 19th-century German painting, and especially the modern French school. Almost all trends of French painting from the Romantic period to the beginning of the 20th century are represented, leading off with Delacroix, the Barbizon landscapists, Corot, Courbet, and followed by the Impressionists Manet, Monet, Pissarro.

In the Museum's first-floor rooms also are canvases by Gauguin, Toulouse-Lautrec, Cézanne, Bonnard and Utrillo; while artists working in more recent styles—Chagall, Vasareli and others—can be seen on the ground floor. Other 19th- and 20th-century schools are more sparsely represented, including works by the German and Austrian painters Waldmüller, Menzel, Leibl, and Kokoschka, by the Italians Favretto and Severini, by Swedish, Polish and other artists.

The Museum's well-known graphics collection consisting of some 10,000 drawings and 100,000 prints is on display only occasionally because of the harmful effects of long exposure to light. A large proportion of these holdings—comprising drawings from the Italian Renaissance and Baroque periods—came to the Museum with the Esterházy Collection, the most outstanding of which are Leonardo da Vinci's red chalk *Head of a Warrior*, along with sketches by Raphael, Correggio, Veronese, Guercino, and Tiepolo, all of ranking importance in terms of world art. There is a large and varied collection of Flemish and Dutch drawings—fifteen by Rembrandt alone—and the German collection is also considerable, including studies by Dürer, Altdorfer and artists from the Danube region. There are also some notable French works, including sheets by Poussin, Watteau and Fragonard, and a large representation of works by 19th- and 20th-century artists: Delacroix, Daumier, Manet, Rodin, Renoir, Cézanne, Degas, and Toulouse-Lautrec.

On the ground floor, the Egyptian collection contains an interesting group of objects pertaining to the Egyptian death cult: mummies, mummiform coffins, sarcophagi, bowls and wooden *ushabty* figures of servants placed in tombs illustrate the art—often of very high quality—all associated with burial customs in ancient Egypt. Also, in addition to objects for everyday use, written records, jewelry, etc. mention should be made of several outstanding sculptures: a large statue of a king from the Middle Kingdom; an exceptionally fine male statue from the New Kingdom (13th century B.C.), a coffer decorated in fine relief, and small bronze figures of animals dating from a later period. Chronologically arranged, the exhibits offer a documented record of the development of Egyptian culture from the Old Kingdom to the Roman conquest.

The Greek and Roman collection was acquired and catalogued quite recently, so that its character and content is to a certain extent affected by this circumstance. Bronze and Iron Age vases are especially noteworthy. The visitor can study the Mycenaean culture and Archaic Greek period through vases, jewelry and terra-cotta statuettes. Besides good Roman copies of Greek sculpture there are a number of outstanding original marbles, notably a well-known Athenian gravestone. There is also a splendid 5th-century B.C. bronze, the famous *Grimani Pitcher*. From the Hellenistic period mention should be made of a marble figure of delicate beauty known as the *Budapest Dancer*, a fine group of Tanagra terra-cotta figurines from the 4th–3rd centuries B.C. and a series of South Italian Red-figure vases. Etruscan art is represented by a wide selection of Black-figure vases—*bucchero*—clay sculptures and other objects; and Roman art, by precious gold jewelry in addition to marble portrait busts that once stood in Roman villas.

The Museum's vast holdings of European sculpture, ranging over almost ten centuries, are distributed in different parts of the building: the medieval and Renaissance pieces are in rooms on the second floor, along the staircase leading to the second floor, and in the Renaissance hall; 17th- and 18th-century works are found in the mezzanine halls; and a collection of 19th- and 20th-century sculptures is accommodated on the ground floor. These collections have been expanded by many new acquisitions, so that there are now examples from virtually every school and period. Its finest section illustrates the development of Italian sculpture. A dramatic *Crucifixion* figure by an artist from Spoleto, a small *Madonna and Child* by Andrea Pisano, and the *Archangel Gabriel* by Agostino di Duccio admirably represent the Italian Trecento and Quattrocento. The works of Lucca della Robbia, Desiderio da Settignano, Benedetto da Majano, and above all the *Christ* by Andrea del Verrocchio, and the *Putto with Dolphin* from his workshop are superb examples of Tuscan Renaissance sculptural expression. Notable examples of the North Italian schools of Padua and Venice include Andrea Riccio's beautiful little bronze, Jacopo Sansovino's monumental Madonna, and works by Alessandro Vittoria and Ticiano Aspetti. But surpassing all of these is the oft-mentioned small bronze *Equestrian Warrior* widely believed to be the work of Leonardo da Vinci. Of special note among the delightful works of the Italian Baroque period are Alessandro Algardi's *Heracles* and bronzes by Francesco Fanelli.

Although not as complete as the Italian, the collection of German and Austrian sculptures provides insights into the works of these countries from the 14th to the 18th centuries. The names of most of the sculptors who worked in stone or wood decorating churches and altars of the early period have remained unknown. But outstanding among the earliest of these are a lovely Virgin Mary from Multscher's workshop, and another *Virgin* possibly by Riemenschneider. The German Renaissance is well represented by Leonhard Kern's *Three Graces*, and the German Baroque and Rococo by several notable works by Meinhard, Guggenbichter, Georg Rafael Donner, Franz Xaver Messerschmidt and others. Noteworthy among the French and Dutch works are a *Saint Barbara* by an artist who worked with Michel Colombe, an *Amor* by Jean Baptiste Pigalle and a bronze by Adriaen de Vries.

The 19th- and 20th-century sculpture collection located on the ground floor offers a fine and detailed overview of individual schools and trends. Outstanding examples of Neoclassicism can be seen in the bas-reliefs of Hans Thorwaldsen and the sculptured portraits of the Austrian Hans Gasser; Romanticism is exemplified by Jean-Baptiste Carpeaux' *Spring*, and Impressionism by the Russian artist Troubetskoy's *Seated Woman*. Auguste Rodin, the greatest sculptor of his time, is represented by six works, including his superb *Eternal Spring*, the *Bronze Age*, and a variation on the well-known *Kiss*. *Portrait of a Woman* by Charles Despiau and a very expressive bronze *Leda* by Aristide Maillol illustrate the development of

14

sculpture in France and the various prevailing trends in the present century. The Museum boasts a notable collection of Belgian works of sculpture, particularly a series dedicated to laborers by Constantin Meunier—*The Smelter* and *The Docker*. In addition to George Minne, another Belgian, one should also mention a few other important artists such as the two Germans Adolf von Hildebrandt and Fritz Cremert, the Finnish sculptor Liipolla, the Yugoslavian Ivan Mestrović, the Italian Medardo Rosso and the Russian Manyizer, each represented by one work. Not long ago the Museum acquired a number of modern works by Emilio Greco, U. Mastroianni, A. Tot, N. Schöffer, E. Hajdu, F. Wotrub and others. Illustrative of the unity and interconnection of modern art, they assume a place in the collection dealing with 20th-century sculpture and painting.

The Museum's permanent and occasional exhibitions and its major treasures have been described in guide books, catalogues and albums, and in foreign-language book series. Two catalogues have been published, one offering full treatment of the Gallery of Old Masters, and the other of its sculpture collection. Periodicals report on research undertaken at the Museum, and readers abroad are acquainted with the *Bulletin du Musée Hongrois des Beaux-Arts*, an art history journal published in Hungarian and French. The Museum also organizes regular lecture series, provides trained guides for different exhibitions and undertakes special study projects.

Considering its outstanding place among the museums of Europe, the Museum of Fine Arts clearly fulfills the goal expressed at the time of its foundation: "It is our wish . . . that this institution should provide a link between past and future, that it should preserve the highest traditions of art, and that it should serve as a basis for further growth and as a renewing source of the ennobling knowledge of art."

ITALY

MASO DI BANCO. *Coronation of the Virgin.*

Within the increasingly ramified Marian iconography of the late Middle Ages, the coronation of the Virgin branched off from the earlier representation of her enthronement, where—symbolizing both the bride from the *Song of Songs,* and the *Ecclesia,* symbol of the Christian church—she is shown seated on a throne at the side of Christ, the bridegroom. This painting in the style of Giotto, on the other hand, presents the Virgin with her head modestly inclined and her arms crossed on her breast, kneeling in front of Christ, who is shown seated on a large Gothic throne intended for both of them, and with both hands placing a pointed crown on her head. The solemn event is assisted by some twenty symmetrically arranged angels with massive golden halos overlapping, and eight angels in the foreground busy playing on various instruments. Many authors have attributed the painting to Maso di Banco, one of the artists whom Vasari combined into one and the same personality, "Tommaso di Stefano, called Giottino." If we judge Maso by the frescoes already attributed to him by Ghiberti (in the Church of Santa Croce, Florence), he was the most gifted of Giotto's pupils. But it is much more difficult to judge him by the altarpieces attributed to him. Stylistically, the ones closest to our *Coronation of the Virgin* are *The Virgin Presenting a Girdle to St. Thomas the Apostle* (Museum Dahlem, Berlin) and *Death of The Virgin* (Musée Condé, Chantilly). It was after the latter that Offner and others have called the author of these three altarpieces "Master of the Chantilly Death of the Virgin," who was probably the young Maso di Banco.

SPINELLO ARETINO. *St. Nemesius and St. John the Baptist.*　　*p. 20*

Spinello Aretino, a successor of Giotto's followers and heirs, had patrons all over Tuscany, and the scope of his work ranged from frescoes with saints' legends and politically colored historical subjects to altarpieces and painted banners. This painting is the left wing of a dismembered triptych for which on 17 April 1384, in Lucca, Spinello Aretino, together with the Florentine carver Simone di Cino and the Sienese gilder Gabriello Saraccini concluded a contract with the prior of the Olivettan monastery of Santa Maria Nuova, Rome, the church where the graves of the two martyrs presented on the two wings, St. Nemesius and St. Lucilla, were venerated. The altarpiece was later transferred to the choir of the monastery church of Monteolivetto Maggiore near Siena, where Vasari saw it. Under the pointed arches of this panel are represented *St. Nemesius*—according to the legend a Roman tribune, and therefore shown as a knight with a sword and a banner—and *St. John the Baptist.* The latter, in the traditional pose of pointing to the infant Jesus, indicates that Christ was represented in the (lost) central panel, and in the quadrifoil above the arches appears *Isaiah,* whose prophecies are frequently quoted as predictions of Christ's birth.

TADDEO DI BARTOLO. *Virgin and Child with St. John the Baptist and St. Andrew.*

p. 20

When this altarpiece was still in its original place, one could read, in addition to the votive inscription on the center panel, the artist's signature and the year: "THADEUS BARTHOLI DE SENIS PINXIT HOC 1395."

18

MASO DI BANCO
Florence, second half of 14th century
Coronation of the Virgin
Tempera on poplar panel, 51.2 × 51.7 cms.
Inv. no. 7793
Gift to the Museum in 1940 from Lord Rothermere, London, who had bought it in London from the dealer P. D. Colnaghi. Probably identifiable with a Coronation of the Virgin ascribed to Giotto and recorded in 1845 in Rome at an auction of the collection of Cardinal Feschi.

The influence most evident in Taddeo's early paintings is that of the great Sienese masters of the first half of the 14th century, the Lorenzetti brothers and Simone Martini. The work here represented gives some indication of the charming Sienese tradition in representations of the Virgin. Even in its 19th-century frame—which shifted the position and sequence of the small figures of saints in the predella—the oversize figures of the Virgin and the Child remain dominant. They combine the older iconographic pattern of the breast-feeding Mother of God (the Byzantine *Galaktotrofousa*) with the new, specifically Sienese variant of the *Madonna dell' Umiltà*, shown sitting on the ground, or alternately—as in our painting—on a cushion on the ground. The pyramidal group of the Virgin and Child is here surrounded by red-winged angels, two of whom are placing a crown on her head. Taddeo di Bartolo, a link between the Sienese Trecento and the International Gothic style of the 15th century, is known for the first undoubted painted self-portrait in West European art.

Upper right
SPINELLO ARETINO
(SPINELLO DI LUCA SPINELLI)
Arezzo circa 1346—Arezzo 1410
St. Nemesius and St. John the Baptist
Tempera on linden panel, 194 × 94.5 cms.
Inv. no. 36.
Gift to the Budapest National Museum from Arnold Ipolyi in 1872. Recorded earlier in the J. A. Ramboux Collection, Cologne. From there the right wing, representing *St. Bernard and St. Lucilla*, went to the Fogg Art Museum, Cambridge, Mass. The frontal piece (*Crowning of the Virgin*) and the predella (*Death of the Virgin*) of the lost central section are preserved in the Pinacoteca Nazionale, Siena; of the paintings on the pilasters of the predella, one is in the Fogg Art Museum, while the remaining two are in the Robert Lehman Collection, Metropolitan Museum of Art, New York.

20

Left
TADDEO DI BARTOLO
Siena circa 1362/63—Siena 1422/23
Virgin and Child with St. John the Baptist and
St. Andrew
Tempera on wood, center panel 114 × 72 cms.;
wings 105 × 43 cms. each; small figures of
saints 39 × 10 cms. each; frame dating from the
19th century.
Inv. no. 53.500.
Painted for the sacristy chapel of the Church of
San Francesco, Pisa, where it remained until the
early 19th century. Subsequent owners: the
Supino family, Pisa; Samuel Festetics and
Friedrich Jakob Gsell, Vienna; Counts Edmund
(Ödön) and Eugen (Jenö) Zichy. In the Museum
since 1953.

SASSETTA (STEFANO DI GIOVANNI)
Cortona circa 1392 (?)—Siena circa 1450
St. Thomas Aquinas Praying at the
Altar of the Virgin (1423–26)
Tempera on poplar panel, 23.6 × 39 cms.
Inv. no. 32.
The painting (left part of a predella) was given
to the National Museum, Budapest, in 1872 by
Arnold Ipolyi. Earlier in the Ramboux
Collection, Cologne. Other panels from the
former triptych are preserved in: Pinacoteca
Nazionale, Siena; Pinacoteca Vaticana; Bowes
Museum, Barnard Castle; Palazzo del
Commune, Massa Maritima; and several private
collections.

SASSETTA (STEFANO DI GIOVANNI). *St. Thomas Aquinas Praying*
at the Altar of the Virgin.

This tiny painting must be imagined as the lower left panel of the seven-part
predella of the great triptych ordered by the Sienese wool-drapers' guild,
the *Arte della lana*, for its chapel in the church of San Pellegrino. The
altarpiece, which was taken apart and sold in the early 19th century, is the
first documented work by the foremost painter of the Sienese Quattrocento.
All is tenderness and purity; and, with the exception of the black cloak of
the Dominican saint, all is brightness as well. The simple Gothic architecture with its artless perspective, verdigris-colored walls and rose-colored
pavement, offers enticing views of the space around the altar, of the garden
with a fountain, and of the monastery library to the right, with the
varicolored bindings of illuminated manuscripts on desks. Even the *Doctor*
angelicus—the great scholastic philosopher who in real life was known for
his corpulence—is presented as a tender and elegant figure. As late as the
15th century, Siena preserved its Gothic character and Berenson, who
reinstated Sassetta to his proper importance, once observed that he painted
as if Florence was forty thousand miles away, and as if Masaccio, Donatel-
lo, Uccello and Castagno had never been born. This is, of course, only
poetic license. In spite of their late-medieval fairy-tale character, Sassetta's
paintings give clear evidence that their creator must have known the work
of Masolino, Masaccio, Fra Angelico, and others.

Left
MICHELE PANNONIO
(MICHELE ONGARO)
Ferrara active from 1415—Ferrara 1459/64
Ceres Enthroned (circa 1450–60)
Tempera on poplar panel, 136.5 × 82 cms.
Signed on the little scroll at foot of throne:
EX MICHAELE PANONIO.
Inv. no. 44.
Donated to the Museum by Arnold Ipolyi in
1880, after Károly Pulszky had discovered it at
the art dealer Ribleto in Florence. Its only
earlier known record is from the Galleria del
Sagro Monte di Pietà, Rome (catalogue of
December 1857).

Facing page
DOMENICO GHIRLANDAJO
(DOMENICO DI TOMMASO BIGORDI)
Florence 1449—Florence 1494
St. Stephen (1490)
Tempera on poplar panel, 191 × 56 cms.
Inv. no. 4914.
Wing of the great altarpiece of the Church of
Santa Maria Novella, Florence, dismantled and
sold in 1804. The most important parts, *The
Virgin and Child with Saints* on the central
panel, and *St. Lawrence* and *St. Catherine of
Siena*, from the wings, are now in the Alte
Pinakothek, Munich. This panel of *St. Stephen*
was owned by Napoleon's brother Lucien
Bonaparte, and later by Duke Talleyrand. Later
recorded in the collection of Edouard Aynard,
Lyons. When auctioned in Paris in 1913, it was
bought by François Kleinberger, who presented
it to the Museum in 1914.

MICHELE PANNONIO. *Ceres Enthroned.* *p. 22*

On a hill rising from a precipitous stony landscape background, a female figure in a pink dress and a gold-embroidered black cloak is shown seated on a highly ornamented throne. Her eyebrows are shaven according to the fashion of the day, and her head is surrounded by halo-like ears of wheat. She holds a grapevine, while above the throne four putti are binding a canopy of apple-twigs. The Greek and Latin inscription on the tablet below indentifies the figure as Ceres, the Roman goddess of agriculture, growth and fertility, equated with the Greek Demeter. Without the inscription we might call the figure simply a personification of *Summer,* or *Abundance,* as indicated in a catalogue of 1857. The signature placed beneath the feet identifes the painter as a certain "Michael of Pannonia," or "Michael the Hungarian," as he was also called. The sparse data on him (i.e., that he worked for the duke Borso d'Este, etc.) confirm what we can already judge from the painting and its harsh sculptural quality, namely that he was close to the School of Ferrara, above all to Cosimo Tura. In connection with our painting one usually mentions Tura's *Spring,* or *Venus,* in the London National Gallery. Probably both paintings—as a cycle of the *Four Seasons,* or in some other context—once served to decorate some *studiolo* in one of the Ferrarese castles. The perspective view of the figures and the thrones, which is common to both paintings, indicates that they were intended for a relatively high place on the wall. Michele Pannonio, who is definitely known only by this picture, was by no means the only link between Hungary and the Early Renaissance in Italy; but his work is certainly the most convincing offspring of the latter, recalling the extensive activities of Italian architects, sculptors, painters and miniaturists for the great Hungarian maecenas, King Matthias Corvinus.

DOMENICO GHIRLANDAJO. *St. Stephen.*

In the third generation of Florentine painters of the 15th century, it was Botticelli who achieved the most exquisite poetry, but Domenico Ghirlandajo who perfected a captivating realism. The last great work executed by Domenico and his extensive workshop was the famous fresco cycle for the choir of the Dominican church of Santa Maria Novella, Florence. For the same patron, the banker Giovanni Tornabuoni, Domenico later worked on a polyptych for the same church, but left it unfinished at his death. Although our *St. Stephen* has been ascribed by some authors to Mainardi, by others to Domenico's brother Davide, there are certain indications that the painting might be from the master's own hand. Vasari's explicit listing of this panel as the work of Ghirlandajo seems supported by the powerful characterization and the use of tempera, which the master's collaborators tended to replace by oil. The plastically modeled figure in a shell-like niche (above which there was originally a tablet with an inscription) represents the first Christian martyr in the traditional diaconal dalmatic, holding a book in his left hand, the martyr's palm in his right, and a stone—the special attribute of his martyrdom—at his feet. The tonsured head is blood-stained, and the face is full of understanding tenderness.

FILIPPINO LIPPI
Prato circa 1457—Florence 1504
St. Anthony of Padua Commending a Friar
to the Patronage of the Virgin
Tempera on poplar panel, 57 × 41.5 cms.
Inv. no. 1140.
Bought for the Museum by Károly Pulszky in
1894 in Venice, from the merchant Luigi
Resimini.

FILIPPINO LIPPI. *St. Anthony of Padua Commending*
a Friar to the Patronage of the Virgin.

Filippino, son of the former Carmelite monk Fra Filippo Lippi and the
beautiful nun Lucrezia Buti, was undoubtedly introduced to painting by his
father; but the elegiac, sensitive work of Botticelli—himself a pupil of Fra
Filippo—exerted a stronger influence on our painter. A comparison between the round-headed, cheerfully earthly Madonnas of Filippo and the
fragile, gracious "Gothic" beings painted by his son, shows that the ideals
must have changed from one generation to the other. No less different is
everything else they portray. A profound earnestness pervades this painting,
even a real sadness, accentuated by the cypress trees at the left edge. Facing

Facing page
CARLO CRIVELLI
Venice 1430/35—Ascoli (?) 1494/1500
Virgin and Child Enthroned, (circa 1476)
Tempera on poplar panel, 106.5 × 55.3 cms.
Signed on the step of the throne:
OPVS. CAROLI. CRIVELLI. VENETI.
Inv. no. 75.
From the Esterházy Collection. Central panel
from the altar of the Dominican Church, Ascoli.
The wing panels (*St. George and the Dragon, St.
Hieronymus, St. Peter Martyr,*
St. Lucy) are now in the National Gallery,
London; earlier they were inserted, by mistake,
into the so-called *Demidov Polyptych.*

OPVS·CAROLI·CRIVELLI·VENETI·

the deeply attentive Virgin Mary, clothed in blue and pink, with downcast eyes and holding the Child on her left knee are the two Franciscan monks, represented in rather traditional fashion, both reduced in scale and in pure profile. The holy intercessor is identified by his usual attribute, the lily, symbol of purity, while his kneeling protégé shows portrait traits, indicating that he was evidently the donor of the painting. Berenson long considered this the work of some unknown painter close to Botticelli, whom he called, in 1899, *Amico di Sandro*. Just as arbitrarily as he had created this unknown fictitious painter, he silently "killed" him in 1932, and on the whole returned this work to Filippino.

CARLO CRIVELLI. *Virgin and Child Enthroned.*   p. 25
Up to the time of Giovanni Bellini, Venice remained an essentially Gothic city. Crivelli, after having been jailed for "abducting" a sailor's wife and living with her, was apparently forced to work outside the city and remained all his life faithful to the conservative trend of Venetian painting, namely the Murano school. The Paduan influence of Squarcione and Mantegna appears here virtually only in the illusionistic foreshortenings. Crivelli's art is marked by extremely precise draughtmansship stressing sculpturesque forms, and by the wealth of gold, richly patterned brocade, architectural details, and *trompe-l'oeil* fruit. As in some of his other paintings, Crivelli was the first to employ plaster relief, as seen in the halos, and in the Virgin's crown, cloak and sleeves in this painting. Notable here is the precise gesture of the Virgin's hand holding the apple, and the attitude of the Child touching the apple in a gesture of benediction. The poignant little Jesus with his painful expression and half-closed eyes, showing a kinship to Mantegna's figures of children, seems to be announcing his future Passion. The significance of the apple could be guessed by any contemporary of the artist: the sin of the First Parents was only redeemed by Christ's Passion and Death.

GENTILE BELLINI. *Portrait of Catherine Cornaro.*   p. 27
Catherine Cornaro (1454–1510) was a Venetian lady from an ancient patrician family, who in 1468 became the spouse of the Cypriote king, James II de Lusignan. On the latter's death in 1489, she "voluntarily" abdicated her kingdom in favor of the Republic of Venice, and thenceforth lived in the castle of Asolo near Treviso, which is still called *Castello della Regina*. Her splendid court there was frequented by poets and scholars, and immortalized by *Gli Asolani*, a set of imaginary Neo-Platonic dialogues on earthly and heavenly love composed by Pietro Bembo. Gentile Bellini also portrayed Catherine in the painting of *The Miracle of the True Cross at the San Lorenzo Bridge* from 1500 (Accademia, Venice). In our portrait she wears the same dress and looks the same age. The artist presents her waist-length against a black background, faithfully rendering not only the jewelry, the veil and the decorations on the dress, but also with candid observation truthfully reproducing the squinting eyes, the double chin and the heavy bodily frame, which nonetheless conveys a total impression of dignity and regal majesty.

26

GENTILE BELLINI
Venice circa 1429—Venice 1507
Portrait of Catherine Cornaro (circa 1500)
Oil on poplar panel, 63 × 49 cms.
A Latin inscription, comprising 8 lines, gives the names of the portrayed lady and the painter.
Inv. no. 101.
Donated to the Budapest National Museum in 1836 by Archbishop László Pyrker, who had bought it in Venice.

GIOVANNI ANTONIO BOLTRAFFIO. *The Virgin and Child.*
This painting by Leonardo's precocious and most talented pupil dates from
the end of the 15th century. There is little doubt that the fifteen-years-older
genius—excitingly present and alive in the Budapest museum's famous
small bronze sculpture of *Warrior on a Rearing Horse*—had a share in this
painting. Here everything is Leonardesque, from the pyramidal composition to the Child's eager features, from the Virgin's facial expression to the
refined shading of the drapery and the extremely precise drawing, which
renders every lock of hair separately . The way in which the infant Jesus
reaches out, with his outstretched hands and with all his body toward
something on the left, in coordinated movement with the Virgin's eyes,
shows that the painting remained, at least in one detail, unfinished. What is
missing is a flower growing from a flowerpot, which is the focus of all these
movements and all this contemplation, and which can actually be found in
certain other paintings from the Leonardo circle, in particular in a painting
of the Virgin and Child in Milan's Poldi Pezzoli Museum.

GIOVANNI ANTONIO BOLTRAFFIO
Milan 1467—Milan 1516
The Virgin and Child
Oil on poplar panel, 83 × 63.5 cms.
Inv. no. 52.
From the Esterházy Collection.

PIERO DI COSIMO. *Volto Santo.*   *p. 30*
This strange painting is based on an unusual subject. A similar representation of Christ on the Cross, clothed in a long, girdled and sleeved tunic, is
found on a venerated Romanesque crucifix in Lucca Cathedral—the so-
called *Volto Santo* (Holy Face), evidently brought over from the Near East.
This extraordinary image of Christ had its origin in the medieval legend of a
bearded female saint, the *Virgo fortis*, or Wilgerfortis. She was pledged to
Christ, but her father, a king of Portugal, wanted to force her into marriage;
and when her prayer for a beard was realized, her father had her crucified.
This legend, which preserves something of the ancient myth of a hermaph-
roditic deity, spread from Spain and the Low Countries all the way to
Poland, Austria, Slovenia and Croatia. In Central Europe the mysterious
saint was best known by her German name of *Heilige Kümmernis.*

The background of this hieratically frontal, oriental object of venera-
tion is a well-articulated, gaily colored landscape, revealing a Tuscan
environment. On the building at the right a tiny figure is painting a fresco of
the Florentine lion (*marzocco*); and on the very right edge we can recognize
the surging outlines of Giotto's Campanile, a part of the cathedral of
Florence.

RAPHAEL. *Portrait of a Young Humanist.* *p. 31*

The unidentified contemplative young man with a tender, oval face and thin-fingered hands resting on the stone parapet is a true Renaissance *bel giovane.* Not only his general appearance and expression, but also the letter in his right hand indicate that he is a humanist intellectual. While there have never been any great doubts about Raphael's authorship, the model has never been definitively identified. At a time when the painting was still the property of the Esterházy family, it was even considered to be a portrait of Raphael by Luini. Later the model was said to be Guidobaldo della Rovere, Duke of Urbino, or an unidentified cardinal, while at present the favorite candidate is Pietro Bembo (1470–1547). This identification is supported by the similarity with the figure on the Bembo medal created some twenty years later by Valerio Belli. The young Raphael could have

Left
PIERO DI COSIMO
Florence circa 1462—Florence 1521 (?)
Volto Santo (early 16th century)
Oil on poplar panel, 160 × 120.5 cms.
Inv. no. 1100.
Ascribed by Gustav Ludwig to Michele da Verona; Bode defined it as belonging to the Venetian school; while Berenson favored Antonio da Solario. First attributed to Piero di Cosimo, by Sándor Lederer. In Piero's opus, the closest parallel is the pair of portraits representing *Giuliano da Sangallo* and *Francesco Giamberti* (cf. *Rijksmuseum/Amsterdam*, pp. 138–139).

RAPHAEL (RAFFAELLO SANTI)
Urbino 1483—Rome 1520
Portrait of a Young Humanist (circa 1504)
Oil on walnut panel, reinforced with pine panel, 54 × 39 cms.
Inv. no. 72.
From the Esterházy Collection.

portrayed Bembo at the Urbino castle, perhaps with the gentle Umbrian landscape in the background. The documented portraits of the young Bembo—including those by Giovanni Bellini and by Titian—have been presumably lost, while the resemblance to the Belli medal is so vague that even the mention by Marcantonio Michiele of a portrait of Bembo by Raphael, who sojourned in Bembo's house in Padua some time about 1530, cannot settle all the doubts. But one thing is certain: it is with this representation of a young humanist that the glorious sequence of Raphael's portraits begins.

RAPHAEL. *The Virgin and Child with the Young St. John the Baptist.*
No artist depicted the Renaissance theme of the Virgin with the two children—the infant Jesus and the *Giovannino*—so frequently, consum-

RAPHAEL
*Virgin and Child with the Young
St. John the Baptist* (circa 1508)
Tempera and oil on poplar panel,
28.5 × 21.5 cms.
Inv. no. 71.
From the Esterházy Collection. According to the inscription on a leaflet on the back of the panel (now missing), Pope Clement XI donated the painting to Elizabeth Christina, wife of Emperor Charles VI. From a later owner, Duke Kaunitz, it was acquired by Prince Miklós Esterházy.

mately and validly as Raphael. The popularity of these creations is proved even by their common appellations, which are still in general use. The Budapest painting, called the *Esterházy Madonna* after its former owners, is of later date than the three most famous versions of the theme, the *Madonna in the Meadow* (cf. *Art History Museum/Vienna,* page 51), the *Madonna with the Goldfinch* (cf. *Uffizi/Florence,* page 95), and the *Beautiful Gardener* (cf. *Louvre/Paris,* page 132). Here the Virgin is shown supporting her son sitting on a rock, while the infant St. John is reading some (invisible) letters on a ribbon. Judging by the ancient Roman ruins in the background, which the preliminary sketch (in the Uffizi) does not show, Raphael continued to work on this painting after his move to Rome in 1508. The state of the entire picture, in particular of the two children,

ANGELO BRONZINO (AGNOLO
DI COSIMO DI MARIANO TORI)
Monticelli 1503—Monticelli 1572
Venus, Cupid and Jealousy (circa 1550)
Oil on poplar panel, 192 × 142 cms.
Signed: *IL BROZINO FIOR F.*
Inv. no. 163.
The painting, once in the collection of Duke
Kaunitz, Vienna, was donated to the Budapest
National Museum in 1863 by Count István
Keglevich.

supports Berenson's opinion that the painting is unfinished, and therefore gives a good insight into Raphael's method of creation. At the same time it represents, in the underlying arrangement of its figures, a further solution to Leonardo's pyramidal composition, which was favored throughout the High Renaissance, but quite particularly developed by its most characteristic genius, Raphael—that master of gentle, but firm, and inexorable balance.

ANGELO BRONZINO. *Venus, Cupid and Jealousy.* *p. 33*

Late Renaissance art stands in contrast to the simple clarity of the Quattrocento, reflecting a time of doubts and unresolved inner conflicts, a time of general social, religious and artistic crisis. The short-lived spiritual balance achieved by the High Renaissance has disappeared, and the tendency is now toward the unusual and the artificial; painting has become ambitious and learned, refined and aristocratic. Bronzino was, from 1540 on, court painter to Cosimo I de Medici, Duke of Florence, and this great allegorical picture is an outstanding example of the complexity and interweaving of coolness

and sensuality in Mannerist art. One could call this painting a simplified version of the even more explicit allegory of the subject preserved in London (cf. *National Gallery/London*, page 58). Venus, holding an arrow, and Cupid, with bow and arrow, are flanked on the right by two putti binding wreaths—perhaps Vasari's *Il Piacere* and *Il Giuoco*—and underneath, by two Satyr masks.

PALMA VECCHIO.
Portrait of a Young Man and *Portrait of a Young Woman*.   *p. 34*
Jacopo Negretti, known as Palma Vecchio is one of the most typical representatives of the contemplative, gently sensuous painting of Venice. Nobody combined so naturally the influences of Giovanni Bellini and Giorgione, in altarpieces of the type of *Sacra Conversazione*, in biblical scenes transposed into pastorals, in mythological figures, and even in portraits. The young man with a red cloak over his armor and an ivy wreath on his head, and the young woman with a grapevine crowning her loosened hair falling over a bared shoulder, have been called a Roman consul and his wife, Mars and Venus, or—the simplest and only correct solution—simply a betrothed couple. The ancient symbolism of the ivy, signifying love and faithfulness, and the vine, representing life, among other things, is self-evident, suggesting that Palma Vecchio painted two figures taken out of the context of their real time and dressed them up *all'antica*.

GIORGIONE (?). *Portrait of a Young Man*.   *p. 36*
One of the favorite paintings in the Budapest Museum is the lyrical portrait of a contemplative youth leaning on a parapet, and looking toward the left. The right hand is pressed against his breast and his outspread fingers point in a direction opposite to that of his eyes. The painting is in a poor state of preservation and what we know about it is problematical. Art historians disagree on even the most elementary questions: is the painter actually Giorgione, as proposed tentatively by Morelli, and as more positively identified by Thausing, Cook, Justi, Fiocco, Pallucchini, Gamba, and— almost to the end—by Berenson? Or is it merely a Giorgionesque work, possibly by Cariani, as Morassi and Heinemann thought? The complexity of the problem is reflected by various other attributions. The name of the man portrayed, Antonio Broccardo, as given by the half-effaced inscription on the parapet, might be of a later date, and therefore itself questionable. The triple-faced female head on the railing, which was considered to be a symbol of the city of Treviso (though it might also represent Hecate or Prudentia), and the black hat with the letter "V," led some authors to believe the painting depicted Vittorio Cappello of Treviso. Lederer, Wickhoff and Auner dated the portrait about 1530, i.e., no less than 20 years after Giorgione's death. Hartlaub thought the signs on the railing represented Masonic symbols. Apparently, this portrait of "Broccardo" is destined to remain forever one of the many mysteries surrounding the life and work of Giorgione.

SEBASTIANO DEL PIOMBO. *Portrait of a Man*.   *pp. 36, 37*
In this masterful High Renaissance portrait the model, in dark clothes and a black beret on his head, is presented half-length, composing a mighty

PALMA VECCHIO
(JACOPO D'ANTONIO NEGRETTI)
Serinalta, circa 1482—Venice 1528
Portrait of a Young Man (circa 1505–08)
Oil on linden panel, 38.7 × 29 cms.
Inv. no. 3460.
Presented to the Museum in 1907 by Baron Richard Hammerstein, Vienna. Prior to that it was in the same collection as the *Portrait of a Young Woman*. It was J. K. Beer who found that the two paintings belong together.

PALMA VECCHIO
(JACOPO D'ANTONIO NEGRETTI)
Serinalta, circa 1480—Venice 1528
Portrait of a Young Woman (circa 1505–08)
Oil on linden panel, 38.8 × 28.5 cms.
Inv. no. 939.
In the collection of Bartolommeo della Nave, Venice, until 1636 (as a work by Giorgione), and from 1638 to 1649 in English hands (lastly the Duke of Hamilton), then in the collection of the Dutch stadholder, Archduke Leopold William; after 1770 at Bratislava Castle, then at Buda Castle, and since 1848 in the Budapest National Museum.

triangle. The grey architecture—the pilaster-articulated wall in the background and the stone block on which the hands are resting—reinforces the monumentality of the whole conception by its system of horizontals and verticals, while the landscape with its light-orange skyline, pervades the picture with a lyrical mood. The painting was long considered the work of Raphael, and the man depicted was most frequently thought to be the poet Antonio Tebaldeo (1463–1537), although his age disagrees with the date of the painting. There is virtually no doubt today that the portrait was painted by Sebastiano del Piombo, a native of Venice, who moved to Rome about 1511 and achieved a perfect harmony between the gentle picturesqueness of Venice and the monumental manner of Rome, a great deal of which is evident in our portrait. The grand-scale Roman, Raphaelesque form here is treated in a picturesque manner, and the mood of the landscape in the background is typically Venetian.

BARTOLOMMEO VENETO. *Portrait of a Man.* *p. 38*
The artist's signature on the painting of his Madonna with Child dated 1502—his last signed work—indicates that he was originally from Venice and Cremona (see *Brera/Milan*, p. 106). Little else is known about his work. There are signs of Bellini's influence although Veneto, especially in his earlier work, uses stronger strokes and firmer modelling. He was evidently attuned to the painting of Leonardo da Vinci and Northern

Lower left
GIORGIONE
(ZORZON DA CASTELFRANCO)
Castelfranco Veneto 1477/78—Venice 1510
Portrait of a Young Man
Oil on canvas, 72.5 × 54 cms.
Inv. no. 94.
Donated to the Budapest National Museum by Archbishop János László Pyrker in 1836. The inscription on the parapet, ANTONIUS • BROKARDUS MAR . . . , may refer to the Venetian poet Antonio Broccardo, who died young in 1531, or to a lawyer of the same name, of whom nothing is known except that he died in 1527.

Below and detail right
SEBASTIANO DEL PIOMBO
(SEBASTIANO LUCIANI)
Venice (?) circa 1485—Rome 1547
Portrait of a Man (circa 1515)
Oil on poplar panel, 115 × 94 cms.
Inv. no. 1384.
Bought at auction by Károly Pulszky from Scarpa di Motta di Livenza collection, Milan, 1895. In the 17th and 18th centuries the painting hung in the Ducal Gallery, Modena.

European art, particularly Dürer. The tradition of the Venetian area is manifest in the *cartellino*, a paper bearing an illegible inscription which very likely gave the name of the painter and perhaps the date. The origins of the *cartellino* have been traced with some certainty to Francesco Squarcione's studio in Padua where apparently each of the numerous apprentices indicated his work with a piece of paper bearing his name until it occurred to someone to paint the piece of paper. Examples of the *cartellino* are first found in Mantegna and other Venetian painters. Green velvet curtains form a background for a bearded, moustachioed man wearing a dark cape with a fur collar, a gold-embroidered cap (*scufietto*) and red beret (berets with ornamental clips are worn by most of Veneto's figures). The face is waxen yellow, the eyes thoughtful, and the whole figure of courtly elegance.

38

BARTOLOMMEO VENETO
Active between 1502 and 1530
Portrait of a Man (circa 1530)
Oil on poplar panel, 51.5 × 42.7 cms.
Inv. no. 2530.
Bought in 1904 at the auction of the Somzée Collection, Brussels, as a work by Sebastiano del Piombo.

LORENZO LOTTO
Venice area 1480—Loretto 1556
Sleeping Apollo and the Muses (1545–1549 ?)
Oil on canvas, 44.5 × 74 cms.
Inv. no. 947.
First ascribed to Lotto by Pigler, who found it
abundantly documented in the artist's *Book of
Sundry Expenses.* At one time in the collection
of the Dutch stadholder, Archduke Leopold
William, Brussels. From Vienna it was
transferred to Bratislava Castle, thence to Buda
Castle, and in 1848 it ended up in the Budapest
National Museum.

LORENZO LOTTO. *Sleeping Apollo and the Muses.*

In a sunlit clearing at the edge of a wood, Apollo is slumbering, with head resting on his arm in a melancholy pose. His bow, his quiver with arrows and his spear are hanging on a tree behind him. The personification of Fame, with a trumpet in her right hand—as described by Cesare Ripa—is shown in full flight, with face averted. In the foreground, the attributes of the Muses—clothes, books, musical instruments, and a globe—are strewn about, while their owners are boisterously splashing about in the brook at the left. The sad allegoric meaning behind this idyll has been defined by the painter himself in his *Libro di spese diverse*: while Apollo sleeps, Fame flies off, and the Muses scatter—signifying that when there is no real guide and protector, the arts degenerate, and the glory departs. Only three or four

39

Muses are visible; but from ancient copies we know that almost a third of the painting was cut off on this side, where all the nine goddesses were originally depicted. The whole concept bears witness to the inventiveness of Lotto, who enriched with original ideas and new compositional devices any kind of painting he attempted, whether figures of saints and biblical scenes, allegories or portraits.

TITIAN. *Doge Marcantonio Trevisani.*

Venetian painting—picturesque and suffused with golden tones—began with Giovanni Bellini, but reached its first indisputable climax in the work of his disciple Titian. This uncontested prince of painting—as he was called—was at the same time Europe's foremost painter of princes. His imperishable portraits have fixed forever the appearance and character of his most eminent contemporaries—from the emperor Charles V and Pope Paul III to kings (Philip II, Francis I) and innumerable cardinals, dukes and other potentates. As official painter of the Republic of Venice from 1517 on (he occupied the sinecure post of *senzale* at the Fondaco de' Tedeschi, which he had impatiently coveted even while Giovanni Bellini was still alive) he portrayed a long succession of doges. One of these was the ailing Marcantonio Trevisani, who became doge in 1553 and died less than a year later. Even beneath the brocade and the velvet, we can sense the feebleness of his body in the unhealthy paleness of his face, the tired look of his watchful eyes, the soft hand pressing the damask handkerchief. This appears to be an unofficial replica—produced partly by the painter's own hand, partly with the help of his workshop—of the official portrait, which probably showed the doge in an ermine coat and which hung in the grand *Sala del Maggior Consiglio* of the Doges' Palace up to 1577, when it was lost in a fire, together with other works by Titian and earlier painters.

TITIAN (TIZIANO VECELLIO)
Pieve di Cadore circa 1480—Venice 1476
Doge Marcantonio Trevisani
Oil on canvas, 100 × 86.5 cms.
Inv. no. 4223.
Bequeathed to the museum in 1912 by Count János Pálffy. Believed to have originated in the Zampieri Collection, Bologna. Later found in Vienna, up to 1859 in the Samuel Festetics Collection; then in the F. Sterne Collection, until its auction in 1886 at O. H. Miethke.

JACOPO BASSANO. *Christ Falling under the Cross.* *p. 42*

In a tumultuous melee of human and animal bodies filling the canvas in a real *horror vacui* up to the white-clouded sky, there is a compulsive movement toward the right. The backs of all the figures bend in the same direction as the arm of the soldier in armor and plumed helmet at upper right. This scene of Christ falling on the way to Mount Calvary, and the woman wiping his face with a cloth—on which according to the legend Christ's "real image," the *vera icon*, was miraculously imprinted, and the woman given the name of St. Veronica, by corruption of the two words—is presented with popular naïveté, yet in the sophisticated idiom of High Renaissance Venetian art. These characteristics—popular subject matter,

formal perfection, and the figures seen from the back—eloquently exemplify Bassano's painting. The poetic group of white-kerchiefed holy women at upper left of this canvas alone would epitomize the characteristic traits that on the one hand link Jacopo's art with his Venetian contemporaries (as well as with Parmigianino and the Florentine Mannerists), and on the other hand served to influence El Greco. In addition to his numerous religious paintings and his portraits, Jacopo Bassano also painted genre pictures, while his sons and his large workshop supplied the market with biblical scenes in genre-like settings and no less homely and rustic "Four Seasons," or "Four Elements."

PAOLO VERONESE. *Portrait of a Nobleman.*

Alongside the traditional Renaissance bust-length portrait of modest dimensions, the 16th century saw the development of more complete figural representation. With increased size and coverage the portrayed person seems physically, and often psychically, remoter from the viewer. The Late Renaissance heroes—emerging after the decline of the short-lived High Renaissance ideals—tend to appear melancholic, if not haughtily misanthropic. The principal exceptions are found in Venice, which because of its social structure and political stability was immune to the catastrophes that ravaged Rome and Florence. The round face of the young Venetian nobleman in this serenely straightforward portrait is far from Bronzino's or

Facing page
JACOPO BASSANO
(JACOPO DA PONTE)
Bassano 1510/18—Bassano 1592
Christ Falling under the Cross (1550)
Oil on canvas, 94 × 114 cms.
Inv. no. 5879.
Gift to the museum in 1922 from Eugen (Jenö)
Boross, New York. Formerly was considered the
work of Andrea Meldolla, called Schiavone
(L. Fröhlich-Bum).

PAOLO VERONESE (PAOLO CALIARI)
Verona 1528—Venice 1588
Portrait of a Nobleman (circa 1560–65)
Oil on canvas, 120 × 102 cms.
Inv. no. 4228.
Bequeathed by Count János Pálffy.

Salviati's rigid, courtly masks. The man stands looking at us with attentive sympathy. He is portrayed knee-length, against a background pervaded with an idyllic mood and divided almost according to the Golden Section: at the left a landscape with a picturesque classical ruin, at the right a wall overgrown with ivy and draped with a heavy red curtain. In spite of the comparatively strict composition all harshness is tempered. Even the gesture of the left arm, held akimbo—which might suggest self-conceit—is given an engaging connotation by the fact that the gloved, elegantly outspread hand is almost nonchalantly pushing the coat away. Formerly ascribed to Moroni, it was the Hungarian scholar Gabor Terey, just before World War I, who first suspected it might be the work of Paolo Veronese.

JACOPO TINTORETTO. *Heracles Chasing a Faun from Omphale's Bed.*
Heracles, who had become effeminate in the service of the Lydian queen Omphale, and exchanged clothes and beds with her before sleeping, with a vigorous kick drove out a faun who had crept into his bed believing there was a woman in it. In the general turmoil Omphale's servants and maids are shown rushing in from all sides. The nocturnal scene is composed in pure diagonals, mainly predetermined by Heracles' body. The varied pos-

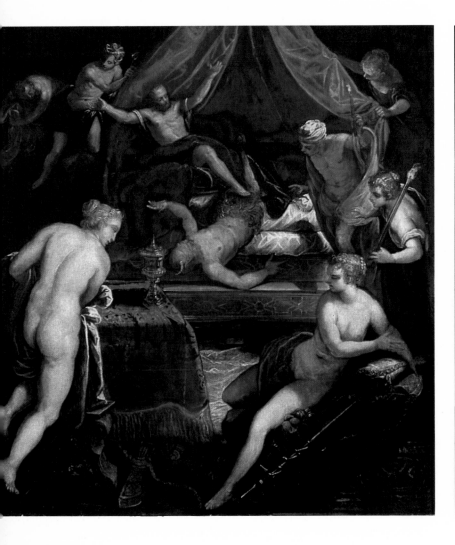

tures and the flickering light recall Ridolfi's report of how Tintoretto studied the distribution of light and shadow on small models made of wax and clay. It is surmised by Klára Garas that the mediator between the artist and his patron the emperor Rudolf II was the antique dealer Ottavio Strada, portrayed by Tintoretto in 1567 (cf. *Rijksmuseum/Amsterdam*, page 143). Strada might also have suggested the subject matter, taken from the Heracles myth described in Ovid's *Fasti* (II, 331–358), although the artist and his contemporaries probably knew it via the scholar Lilio Gregorio Giraldi's book *Ercole*, published in Modena in 1557. Both Giraldi and Ridolfi refer to Iole instead of Omphale, a frequent confusion in Renaissance literature.

BERNARDINO LUINI. *Virgin and Child with St. Catherine and St. Barbara.*   *p. 44*

Of all the influences evident in Luini's painting—Leonardo, Foppo, Bergogno, Solario, Bramantino and the Umbro-Tuscan school—the most prominent is that of Leonardo, although Bernardino's borrowings are rather superficial, as can be seen in the Leonardesque facial types of our painting. Yet he is, next to Boltraffio, the only Lombard painter whose religious paintings show some High Renaissance greatness and harmony. The central figure, protectively holding the little Jesus, has an inscription on the border of her red dress: VIRGINIS MATER. But it is evident that the woman depicted is not St. Ann, but the Virgin Mary. The two saints at either side—the virgin-martyrs St. Catherine of Alexandria and St. Barbara—are among the most revered *virgines capitales*, known as the "fourteen helpers in need." In addition to their palms of martyrdom, they are identified by their special attributes: the red-haired and red-robed Catherine wears the wheel of her torture embroidered on the neckline of her dress, while Barbara's olive-green dress shows the image of the tower where she was imprisoned by her malicious father. The Christ Child standing on a stool is turning over the leaves of a prayer book with black and red writing, golden edges and a black binding.

GIROLAMO ROMANINO. *Portrait of a Man.*   *p. 46*

The Brescian painter Girolamo Romanino attempted various subjects, both in frescoes and panel-paintings; but he has remained alive for us chiefly as a portrait painter. This handsome work dates from the period when the artist's main inspirations were Giorgione and Titian. In front of a green velvet curtain we see the half-length figure of a man with his hand clutching a sword-hilt. On his head is a *balzo*, a fashionable round cap worn by both men and women, and the white shirt with the embroidered collar is covered by a gold-brocaded robe. This gorgeous costume, however, is subordinated to the psychologically acute rendering of the face. Despite the martial implication of the weapon, the sword is resting in irresolute hands, and the model seems to be squinting, a defect which Romanino skillfully balances between representing and half-disguising (recalling Raphael's earlier portrait of *Cardinal Tommaso Inghirami*). The absent-minded expression and the deviant eyes seem to be set far from the real world, in Saturn's *vita contemplativa* rather than in Jupiter's *vita activa*.   45

Far left
JACOPO TINTORETTO
(JACOPO ROBUSTI)
Venice 1518—Venice 1594
Heracles Chasing a Faun from Omphale's Bed (circa 1582–84)
Oil on canvas, 112 × 106 cms.
Inv. no. 6706.
Probably belongs to Tintoretto's series of four representations of the Heracles myth (cf. *National Gallery/London*, page 68), painted for the Emperor Rudolf II. In the 17th century, owned by the Duke of Buckingham; acquired at auction in Antwerp in 1648 by Archduke Leopold William for his brother, Emperor Ferdinand III. Preserved at Prague Castle (inventory from 1685) and later at the Vienna Kunsthistorisches Museum. In 1932 the Venice agreement assigned it to Hungary, and the Budapest Museum took it over in 1934.

BERNARDINO LUINI
Luino circa 1480/90—Milan 1531/32
Virgin and Child with St. Catherine and St. Barbara
Oil on poplar panel, 94 × 72 cms.
Inv. no. 58.
From the Esterházy Collection.

ROMANINO (GIROLAMO ROMANO)
Brescia 1484–87—Brescia 1559 or later
Portrait of a Man (circa 1520)
Oil on poplar panel, 82.5 × 71.5 cms.
Inv. no. 1254.
Bought by Károly Pulszky in Venice in 1895.
Originally in the Palazzo Fenaroli, Brescia; then
in the Achille Glisenti Collection in the
same city.

CORREGGIO. *Madonna del Latte.*   *p. 47*

Goethe's *Travels Through Italy* mentions a painting by Correggio that
represents the weaning of the Christ Child, hesitating between his mother's
breast and a pear offered to him, and wondering which to choose. "Yes,"
remarks Goethe "this is a picture! It contains wit, naïveté, sensuality, all at
one and the same time. The holy object has become plainly human, valid as
a symbol of a stage in life we all are bound to experience. Such a painting is
eternal, for it reaches back to the earliest times of humanity, and forward
into the future . . ." On the basis of this description, our painting depicting
the Virgin with the Child and an Angel (who could well be the infant John
the Baptist, were it not for the wings) can be supposed to be the painting
Goethe admired in Naples in 1787. The word "suppose" must be emphasized, for already the critic Corrado Ricci, who considered the Budapest
painting to be the original, counted some twenty early copies. The picturesque, gently sensual Correggio was particularly popular in the 18th century, when quite typically, the painter Anton Raphael Mengs was named at
his birth first of all after Correggio (Antonio Allegri), and only secondarily
after Raphael.

CORREGGIO (ANTONIO ALLEGRI)
Correggio near Parma 1489—Correggio 1534
Madonna del Latte (circa 1524–26)
Oil on poplar panel, 68.5 × 56.8 cms.
Inv. no. 55.
From the Esterházy Collection. In the late 18th
century (1795 ?) the painting was bought by
Miklós Esterházy from the Duke of Crivelli in
Naples; the latter had obtained it from his
uncle, Cardinal Crivelli, to whom it is supposed
to have been given by a king of Spain, perhaps
Charles III.

47

ANNIBALE CARRACCI. *Christ and the Samaritan Woman at the Well.*
The Old Testament scenes of Rebecca and Eliezer and of Jacob and Rachel at the well are paralleled in the New Testament by the encounter of Christ and the Samaritan Woman (John 4, 7–27). In this painting, Christ's disciples show various degrees of astonishment at overhearing their master's conversation with the woman. The figures are shown full of inner dignity, with deliberate and restrained gestures, in the Arcadian setting of a beautiful landscape where the shadows are lengthening, and the day pointing toward the evening.

Roman painting around 1600 is marked on the one hand by the impetuous Caravaggio, and on the other, by the more classically–minded Carraccis. This picture was intended for Perugia and painted at the time when the artist was decorating the Farnese Palace in Rome, for Cardinal Odoardo Farnese. The figures reveal how much of Raphaelesque beauty the founders of the Bologna School managed to carry over into their own time. The background represents one of the first attempts at idealized landscape,

ANNIBALE CARRACCI
Bologna 1560—Rome 1609
*Christ and the Samaritan Woman
at the Well* (circa 1597)
Oil on canvas, 76.5 × 63.5 cms.
Inv. no. 3823.
Painted for the Benedictine church of San
Pietro, Perugia. Later recorded in the Six
Collection, Amsterdam; in the collections of
Marquis de Seignelay and Duke Philippe
d'Orléans, Regent of France; in the S. Clarke
and G. Hibbert collections, England; and in
Prague (G. Hoschek von Mühlheim). Bought for
the museum at J. Goudstikker, Amsterdam, in
1908.

an innovation pioneered by Annibale, Paul Bril and Adam Elsheimer. What the 19th-century critic Gian Pietro Bellori admired so much in Annibale's paintings is his fusion of Roman *disegno* with Venetian colorism.

GIUSEPPE CESARI. *Diana and Actaeon.*
The goddess Diana, angry at being observed while bathing with her nymphs, transformed the hunter Actaeon into a stag, and he was promptly devoured by her hounds. Giuseppe Cesari was Caravaggio's teacher but—in contrast to his headstrong pupil—he was a confirmed eclectic. Here he obligingly displays a cave and a pond in front of it where Diana and her attendants are represented in five variations on the theme of the female nude. Cesari, whose patrons included several popes and two kings of France, painted frescoes and altarpieces, besides unpretentious scenes like this present one, which pleased everyone. But they give not the slightest foretaste of the great reform carried out by the Carraccis, and even less of the overwhelming revolution effected by his pupil, Caravaggio.

GIUSEPPE CESARI (CAVALIER D'ARPINO)
Frosinone 1568—Rome 1640
Diana and Actaeon
Oil on copper, 50 × 69 cms.
Signature on the stone in front of Actaeon's foot.
Inv. no. 508.
From the Esterházy Collection. A replica is preserved in the Louvre.

49

GUIDO RENI. *David and Abigail.*

On one side we see David, a young commander, in full armor, standing with his right arm akimbo. Facing him we see Abigail, seated sidesaddle on a donkey. The wise, clever and humbly inclined face of the petitioner in this canvas shows the painter's familiarity with the Christian tradition, already well established in medieval typology, according to which Abigail, that paragon of womanly cleverness and diplomacy, was a precursor of the Virgin Mary. Guido Reni was in his lifetime renowned throughout Europe, but the judgments on the School of Bologna have changed considerably. Soon one began to reproach the sweetness and sentimentality of his figures, although this was to some extent the fault of the numerous copies and imitations. Supporting the belief that it is the work of Reni's own hand is the exceptionally reliable history of the painting and the presence of *pentimenti*—i.e., corrections carried out in the course of the work—unknown in any of the copies.

FRANCESCO FURINI. *Venus Mourning the Death of Adonis.* *p. 51*

The Adonis myth is preserved in Theocritus and Ovid (Met. X, 708–728), and was popularized by Marino's poem *Adone* (1623). Furini's treatment of

GUIDO RENI
Bologna 1575—Bologna 1642
David and Abigail
Oil on canvas, 153 × 161 cms.
Inv. no. 490.
Owned by the Praun family, Nuremberg; at that time (1738) the painting was copied in a copper plate etching by Johann Martin Preisler. Paul Praun, the first owner of the picture, knew Reni, and it was from his descendants that it was acquired by the Esterházys. A version of the painting is in New York (Walter P. Chrysler, Jr. Collection).

50

the subject—created only two years later—is suspended between the theatrical despair of Venus and the quiet, submissive sadness of her attendants around the body of her lover, gored by a boar as he was hunting. The broken bow on the ground and the putto with the expiring torch complete the image of a tragic end.

It is Furini's first large-scale work but even here we can suspect what is the actual core of his art: little more than a painfully sensitive revival of slender female nudes, modeled in gentle *sfumato* and suffused by a cold light. Furini's obsession with sensuality makes it difficult to imagine him living and acting as a priest in later life. Yet he is one of the very few Florentine masters of the period who cannot be overlooked.

FRANCESCO FURINI
Florence around 1600—Florence 1646
*Venus Mourning the Death
of Adonis* (circa 1625)
Oil on canvas, 233 × 190 cms.
Inv. no. 493.
From the Esterházy Collection. Baldinucci
reports that the painting was commissioned by
the Florentine merchant Giovanni Battista
Baccelli.

SALVATOR ROSA. *Seaport.*

We are shown a harbor view that could well serve as the setting for some pirate's tale. In a small, irregular cove among wild rocks and picturesque ruins can be seen several sailing ships and boats lying at anchor, with people bustling around on board. Until quite recently the painting was dated in the mid-18th century and ascribed to some unidentified successor of Andrea Locatelli. But restoration has proved that the signature ROSA is genuine, and Garas has justifiably pinned down the painting to the artist's Florentine period, when Rosa was especially influenced by Claude Lorrain's idyllic harbors. Earlier the self-willed Rosa had become well known as a painter of battle scenes, which he successfully continued to develop from his teacher, Falcone, whose special domain this was, and a large proportion of his paintings is devoted to mysteriously terrifying, biblical, mythological and other scenes from antiquity, or allegories that were often puzzling even to his contemporaries. Rosa, a painter, graphic artist, poet, musician and

SALVATOR ROSA
Arenella, near Naples 1615—Rome 1673
Seaport (circa 1641–47)
Oil on canvas, 87.5 × 111 cms.
Signed at lower center.
Inv. no. 535.
Acquired by Ferdinand Charles, Archduke of Tyrol, from the painter's friend Francesco Cordini. It hung in the collection at Ambras Castle, whence it was transferred to the imperial collections in Vienna and later to Buda Castle.

actor, whom the imagination of the 18th century also endowed with sword
and dagger, showed a predilection for depicting Nordic ghosts and witches,
whose pedigree leads back to Dürer and Baldung.

MARCO LIBERI. *Jupiter and Mnemosyne.*
Jupiter, the mightiest and wisest of all the gods of antiquity, was an
insatiable lover, whose taste ranged from goddesses to humans—a real
"father of gods and men," who begot half of the Olympians and a huge
number of mortals. The painters, who could hardly be supposed to follow
all the innumerable *amori di Giove*, preferred to concentrate on the fate of
earthly maidens: Europa, whom he abducted as a bull; Danaë, whom he
visited in the form of a golden rain; Leda, whom he loved as a swan; Io,
whom he embraced transformed into a cloud; Antiope, whom he seduced as
a Satyr; and others. Here Marco Liberi, son of the better-known Venetian
painter Pietro Liberi, depicts Jupiter as a brown eagle descending toward
the fair-haired Titanid Mnemosyne, goddess of memory, with whom he was
to beget, in nine nights, the nine Muses. The diagonally composed painting
is one of the rare signed works by this little known artist, who is here,
according to the opinion of some authorities, approaching the style of his
younger contemporary, Antonio Bellucci.

SEBASTIANO RICCI. *Moses Defending the Daughters of Jethro.* *p. 54*
Ricci, a "typical 18th-century virtuoso extrovert," as defined by Wittkower,
was an ambitious artist, covetous of glory and money and always desirous
of satisfying his patrons, whom he found among the cream of European
society. Having become well acquainted with the art of Annibale Carracci

MARCO LIBERI
Padua 1640—unknown locality, after 1725
Jupiter and Mnemosyne
Oil on canvas, 118 × 153 cms.
Signed on the sheet of music on the left.
Inv. no. 616.
From the Esterházy Collection. Sold to the
Esterházys in 1816 by Dániel Kászonyi.

and the masters of Roman baroque illusionism, in particular Paolo Veronese and Luca Giordano, he tended to imitate their manners, to a degree that verges on plagiarism. This applies quite particularly to this ostensibly Giordanesque painting. The biblical subject of the young Moses (Exodus 2, 16–17) protecting the seven daughters of his future father-in-law and scattering the shepherds who had molested them at the well, had several pictorial antecedents in the Renaissance period, notably those by Botticelli (cf. *Vatican Museums/Rome*, page 67) and by Rosso Fiorentino (cf. *Uffizi/ Florence*, page 114). In Ricci's picture the whole scene is impressively

staged as in a good theatre. Two of Jethro's beautiful daughters are shown struck with wonder and admiration while Moses with a club, Heracles-like, is driving out the panic-stricken intruders.

ALESSANDRO MAGNASCO. *Torture-Chamber.*   *p. 55*

When the Genoese painter Magnasco sojourned in Florence in the early 18th century, he became acquainted in the Medicean capital with the paintings of Salvator Rosa and the prints of Jacques Callot. It was on these

two artists, long since dead, but still highly influential, that he founded his

SEBASTIANO RICCI
Belluno 1659—Venice 1734
*Moses Defending the Daughters
of Jethro* (circa 1720–30)
Oil on canvas, 114 × 178 cms. (trimmed on all the edges).
Inv. no. 57.10.
Presented to the Museum in 1957 by the wife of Josef Csetenyi, Budapest. The preliminary sketch is preserved at the Accademia, Venice.

own style of painting and his own, unmistakable, somber and grotesque world of fancy. The picture here reproduced takes some details from Callot, but the total impression is distinctly Magnasco's own. In a spacious room with barred windows our eyes move in terror from the executioners, soldiers, judges and interrogators to the victims waiting in their chains, undergoing torture, or dropping on the ground after experiencing torments. The same tiny, puppetlike, long-limbed figures without any individual traits taking part in the gruesome game of Counter-Reformational inquisition (a painting of the crucified Christ is hanging on the wall as a mockery of all

ALESSANDRO MAGNASCO
(LISSANDRINO)
Genoa 1667—Genoa 1749
Torture-Chamber
Oil on canvas, 44 × 85 cms.
Inv. no. 594.
From the Esterházy Collection.

that is happening in its view) can be found in other paintings by Magnasco. In the flickering light of monastery refectories and libraries, soldiers' bivouacs, storm-tossed landscapes, synagogues and ruins we can discern monks, nuns and soldiers, Don Quixotes and St. Anthonys of Padua, beggars and comedians, gypsies and flagellants—all a repeated image of diabolical mockery and inescapable decadence, all reflecting the same depressing and morbid hallucination of guilt and penance, of ecstatic prayer and no less ecstatic bacchanalia, of immense poverty, immense injustice and boundless superstition, all in Magnasco's increasingly daring, quick-stroked *al tocco* technique.

Left
GIOVANNI BATTISTA TIEPOLO
St. James the Greater (circa 1757–58)
Oil on canvas, 317 × 163 cms.
Signed on the sword on the ground.
Inv. no. 649.
From the Esterházy Collection. Prince Miklós
Esterházy bought the painting from Edmund
Burke, together with some other pictures of
Spanish origin.

GIOVANNI BATTISTA TIEPOLO
Venice 1696—Madrid 1770
The Virgin Mary with Six Saints
(circa 1755–56)
Oil on canvas, 72.8 × 56 cms.
Inv. no. 651.
Donated to the Budapest National Museum in
1836 by János László Pyrker, as a work by
Gregorio Lazzarini.

GIOVANNI BATTISTA TIEPOLO. *St. James the Greater.* *p. 56*

Throughout the Middle Ages and even later, it was firmly believed that the apostle James the Greater had preached the Gospel in Spain and was buried on Spanish soil. It followed that Santiago de Compostela became, next to Rome and Jerusalem, the greatest goal of pilgrimage. It was even claimed that the apostle appeared to King Ramiro and his Christian warriors at the battle of Clavijo, riding a white horse with sword in hand and helping them to defeat the Saracens. In keeping with this legend of St. James as *Santiago Matamoros*—the "Moor-Killer," it is almost certain that this great altarpiece by Tiepolo was produced, if not in Spain (as was thought at one time), at least for a Spanish patron. In engaging contrast with the violent subject matter, the painting is distinguished by a luminous harmony of whites, pale-yellows, light-blues, and the pink and reds of the rider's flag, which dominate the darker and cooler tones at lower left. The saintly rider, casually decapitating the dark-skinned infidel, is shown on the crest of a hill, with eyes raised to the sky toward two rosy-hued angels who look on approvingly.

GIOVANNI BATTISTA TIEPOLO. *The Virgin Mary with Six Saints.* *p. 57*

Eighteenth-century Venice, although hopelessly decayed politically, reached a new height in her painting. In creative activity which spread to many parts of Italy and beyond, she produced the last great universal genius whose works combine Baroque magnificence with the playful elegance of Rococo and a magisterial coolness presaging the approach of Neo-Classicism. The virtuoso Giambattista Tiepolo painted with absolute mastery practically everything: illusionistic frescoes, altarpieces, mythological scenes, ancient history, Ariosto's *Orlando furioso* and Tasso's *La Gerusalemme liberata*, apotheoses, allegories, portraits. This canvas was produced for some unknown patron, at a time when he had already completed his famous work in Würzburg. On a cloud, in front of two mighty Doric columns with a moss-covered cross alongside, the Virgin is represented as the *Immaculata*, in radiant light and with a snake beneath her feet. Below her is seen a group of saints in various attitudes, among whom can clearly be recognized St. Joseph with his flowering rod, St. Teresa of Avila, and St. Francis bending over the symbols of death. At extreme left, dressed in light red under a cloak of royal blue, stands St. Louis of France. But positive identification of all these personages is relatively unimportant. All antitheses have been assimilated in the artist's vision—reality and fancy, heaven and earth, sensual vision and religious pathos—have become subordinated to the all-embracing interplay of light and color, and gentle, evanescent outlines.

BERNARDO BELLOTTO. *The Arno in Florence with Santa Trinità Bridge.* *p. 59*

The *veduta*, or topographically exact depiction of a specific locality, townscape or architecturally defined landscape, was known from the late Middle Ages on, first in such examples as the calendar miniatures in the famous Book of Hours of the Duke of Berry, and later with views in true perspective. Except for the rich contribution of graphic art, notably in Piranesi's

BERNARDO BELLOTTO
Venice 1721—Warsaw 1780
*The Arno in Florence with
Santa Trinità Bridge* (circa 1742)
Oil on canvas, 62 × 90 cms.
Inv. no. 647.
From the Esterházy Collection.

Roman views, it must be noted that this branch of painting flourished notably in two periods and picturesque environments, 17th-century Holland and 18th-century Venice. In Venice its most successful practioners were Canaletto, Francesco Guardi and Bernardo Bellotto—the latter was also called Canaletto after his uncle. On the whole Bellotto was more true to life in his "mirror images" of the actual world than his uncle; therefore it is due to him that we know pretty exactly how Turin, Vienna, Dresden, Munich and Warsaw looked in the mid-18th century. This view of the Arno River was painted from the famous Ponte Vecchio. We are looking in the direction of the water current, all the way to the Santa Trinità Bridge, beyond which we can discern the outlines of the Ponte alla Carraia. Among the mass of buildings on the banks can be clearly distinguished the rectangular fortified turrets dating from the Middle Ages, which have proved their solidity and survived even the inglorious retreat of the Germans at the end of World War II.

59

BERNARDO BELLOTTO. *Piazza della Signoria, Florence.*

This view of the civic center of Florence offers a faithful, clear and poetic image of its appearance at the time when the Medici dynasty had just come to an end. In this proud and solemn setting the Gothic towers still dominate everything, from left to right, the belfry of the Badia, the Bargello, and highest of all, the tower of the town hall, the so-called *Palazzo della Signoria*, later known as the Palazzo Vecchio (after the Medicis had moved to the Pitti Palace on the other bank of the Arno). We can also recognize several celebrated monuments: aligned on the left are Giambologna's equestrian statue of Cosimo I and Ammanati's *Neptune Fountain*; and in front of the Palazzo Vecchio the two colossal statues, Bandinelli's *Heracles* and Michelangelo's *David*. On the right we recognize the Loggia de' Lanzi, and beneath its nearest arch is the most famous example of spiraling Mannerist sculpture, Giambologna's *Rape of a Sabine*. The total impression is enlivened by a golden coach drawn by black horses and attended by a red-liveried coachman.

60

BERNARDO BELLOTTO
Piazza della Signoria, Florence (circa 1742)
Oil on canvas, 61 × 90 cms.
Inv. no. 645.
This painting, a *pendant* to the preceding one, belonged to the Esterházy Collection from 1819 to 1870, and was at that time considered to be by Canaletto.

SPAIN

EL GRECO. *Penitent Magdalen.*

The first really great Spanish painter was—as his name *El Greco* indicates—a Greek immigrant from Crete who moved to Venice and studied under Titian. Then in Rome he was patronized by the miniaturist Giulio Clovio and it was probably in the hope of obtaining orders from Philip II for the decoration of the Escorial that he came to Spain. He thus became not merely a link between three cultures—Byzantine, Italian and Spanish—but also between two ages, the Late Renaissance, particularly in its Mannerist period, and the Baroque. He was rediscovered toward the end of the last century by the Spanish art historian Manuel Cossio and, with the development of Expressionism, his work conquered the world.

In this painting of the *Penitent Magdalen,* dating from soon after he had moved to Spain, we can still discern certain traits that link El Greco

EL GRECO
(DOMENIKOS THEOTOKOPOULOS)
Fodele, Crete, 1541—Toledo 1614
Penitent Magdalen (circa 1580)
Oil on canvas, 156.5 × 121 cms.
Inv. no. 564.
The painting was at one time in the Ivan Shchukin Collection, Paris. Gift to the museum in 1921 from Marcell Nemes.

EL GRECO
The Annunciation (circa 1600–1605)
Oil on canvas, 91 × 66.5 cms.
Signed (in Greek) *Domenikos Theotokopoulos*
Inv. no. 3537.
The painting once hung in the collection of the Marquis de Rochefort, Paris. It was sold to the Museum in 1907 for the sum of 20,000 francs by the Paris art dealer François Kleinberger. Of the many variants the closest is at the Museum of Art, Toledo (Ohio, USA); a further close variant is in São Paulo (cf. *Art Museum/São Paulo,* page 117).

with Venice (where he first met this subject). But even here—before he painted his great *Funeral of Count Orgaz*—we can distinguish the features that are peculiarly characteristic of him, notably the strident disharmony of yellow and blue tones, which bear no relation to the resonant warmth of the Venetians. When the painting was created, Spain's greatest 16th-century mystics, St. Teresa of Avila and St. John of the Cross, were still alive; and El Greco himself was destined to become the greatest mystic of painting.

EL GRECO. *The Annunciation.* *p. 63*

By the end of the 16th century Domenikos Theotokopoulos had become a pure visionary. In this painting dating from ca. 1600, he shapes the traditional, seemingly exhausted theme of the Annunciation into a mighty vision, far from any semblance to ordinary life. The grey-blue background is torn apart by a cascade of light, centered in the hovering dove of the Holy Spirit. The carmine-red robe of the Virgin, who looks up thoughtfully from her reading, and the yellowish-brown clothing of the archangel Gabriel, descending toward her with his right hand raised, introduce into this supernatural world two independent, yet at the same time interconnected and equally mysterious color accents. All that remains of the Virgin's earthly surroundings—as on a stage, whose real dimensions are distorted by the spotlights—are the bookstand with prayer book, the sewing basket and the vase of flowers. Everything else, merging with the two protagonists, is inaccessible and exalted, transfigured both corporeally and formally into the rapturous experience of a mystery.

EL GRECO. *The Agony in the Garden.*

In this late work, reality has changed into feverish vision, the apparitions have become increasingly arbitrary, but have thereby achieved an inner consistency, linking every smallest detail.

Eerily illuminated as if by a flash of lightning, the vertically composed scene of Christ's agony on the Mount of Olives ominously announces the approaching storm. Near the top, Christ praying in deep anguish (Matthew 26, 36–46) represents the peak of an isosceles triangle whose base-line is formed by the sleeping apostles, the young St. John the Evangelist, St. James the Elder and St. Peter. Facing the kneeling God-man—the color of whose clothing, nowhere else repeated, is the real focus of the composition—we see a brilliantly illuminated angel at the left, kneeling on a cloud and offering the chalice of suffering (Luke 22, 43). On the right, in the distance, in cool flickering light, the soldiers are approaching; and further away can be seen the city of Jerusalem.

El Greco's phantasmagorias, whose features some authorities have prosaically and wrongly attempted to attribute to the painter's astigmatism, are to the last detail dictated by an inner vision. As in a nightmare, all the components are curiously interrelated, yet at the same time sharply distinct and independent. The barren landscape accentuates the figural arrangement, and the figures themselves are interconnected entities, as are the twisted, half-withered, half-greening trees and bushes surrounding the apostles.

EL GRECO
The Agony in the Garden, (circa 1605–1610)
Oil on canvas, 170 × 112.4 cms.
Signed: *Domenikos Theotokopoulos*
Inv. no. 51.2827.
Probably from Sigüenza Cathedral. Recorded in the Marcell Nemes Collection; later owned by Leopold (Lipó) M. Herzog. In the Museum since 1951.

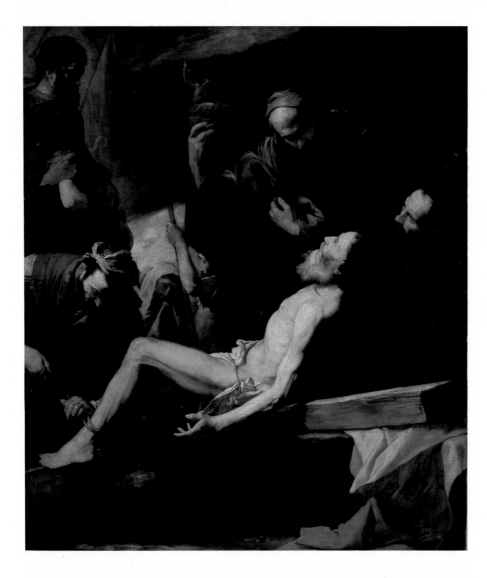

JUSEPE DE RIBERA (LO SPAGNOLETTO)
Játiva (Valencia) 1591—Naples 1652
The Torture of St, Andrew
Oil on canvas, 209 × 183 cms.
Signed at lower right and dated 1628.
Inv. no. 523.
From the Esterházy Collection. Earlier in the
collection of Duke Kaunitz, Vienna.

JUSEPE DE RIBERA. *The Torture of St. Andrew.*   *Above, and detail right*
The influence of Caravaggio's *chiaroscuro* and his no less powerful realism
can be observed in almost all European painting of the first half of the 17th
century, particularly in Southern Italy and Spain. Ribera's art, which
belongs to both these regions, is of exceptional importance for the later
development of painting, for he in turn influenced not only Italians—like
Luca Giordano—but also Spaniards. In addition to mystic rapture, the
favorite subject was cruel torture, which allowed the painter to unleash his
darker instincts, while giving a pleasurable shudder to the believers contemplating such a picture in church. Ribera, who supplemented his tortures of
saints with no less terrifying tortures of mythological figures (*Apollo
Flaying Marsyas*) was even in this respect a child of his time. The *Torture of
St. Andrew*, which can be compared to Caravaggio's *Crucifixion of St. Peter*
in the church of Santa Maria del Popolo, Rome, is an excellent example of
this art. The illumined parts of the bodies, especially the saint's diagonal
nude figure, seem to be literally tearing themselves out of darkness; they
prove Ribera's perfect knowledge of anatomy and his painstaking truthfulness to the model; but they are at the same time subordinated to a higher,

Facing page
JUSEPE DE RIBERA (LO SPAGNOLETTO)
The Torture of St. Andrew, detail

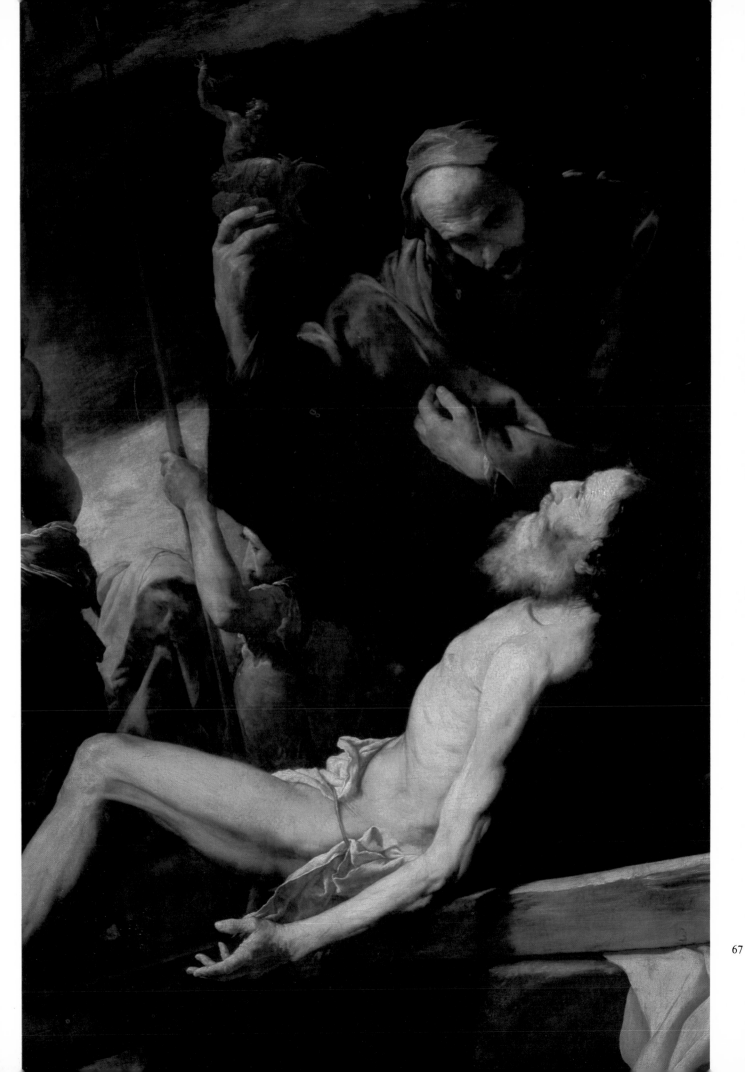

and unquestionably monumental arrangement of the whole. While St. Andrew is being tied to the cross, the somber-hued pagan priest is once again showing an idol, the figure of Jupiter, to the saint expected to worship him. This was an object lesson for any believer, up to the point of exciting religious fanaticism.

FRANCISCO DE ZURBARÁN. *St. Andrew the Apostle.*
This "Spanish Caravaggio," seven months older than Velázquez and almost twenty years senior to Murillo, constitutes with these two the glittering three-star constellation of the *Siglo de Oro*—an expression that has begun to be applied not merely to the literature, but also to the painting of 17th-century Spain. The core of Zurbarán's art consists of monumental, mostly full-length figures of saints, along with entire cycles of sacred legends, usually executed for provincial monasteries. The few independent still-lifes and portraits he managed to paint in addition are in no respect inferior to his religious paintings, which are characterized by sculpturesque form and ascetic fervor. His quiet, unworldly spirituality disguised under the appearance of realism becomes lucid even in his most everyday subjects. This portrayal of St. Andrew absorbed in reading shows a mighty figure dominating the entire foreground, an austere, uncompromising personage, modeled with Caravaggiesque earthiness, a man seemingly impervious to smiles or tears. Yet despite its truthfulness to life and its evident links to the real world, this masterpiece is an image of spiritual rather than material life. The philosophy of St. Thomas Aquinas, according to which physical objects are merely *spiritualia sub metaphoris corporalium*, pervades Zurbarán's intensely personal vision of the world and its order.

FRANCISCO DE ZURBARÁN. *The Immaculate Conception.*   *p. 69*
The Virgin, golden-haired and dressed in white, with a pink girdle and a blue cloak spreading like a sail in the wind, is shown with her eyes turned up to heaven, at the time miraculously hovering above earth and rising like the dawn—*ut aurora consurgens* (Song of Songs, 6, 10). It is a Christianized version of the Bride from the Song of Songs, a vision of spotless beauty—*tota pulchra*. Her head is surrounded by a diadem of twelve stars—sign of the apocalyptic woman clothed with the sun—and by a faint halo, while five little angel heads cluster at her feet. Far down to the right we can recognize the proud city of Seville, dimly glimmering through the radiant haze; and in the clouds around her can be seen the well-known symbols of the Virgin's immaculate purity, which the theologians have borrowed from the Song of Songs, the Book of Wisdom, Sirach and other Biblical passages, rendered in translucent figurations.

The Immaculate Conception—in Spanish, *La Inmaculada Concepcion,* or *La Purisima*—was one of the favorite subjects of Baroque painters throughout Europe, and had a special following in ultra-Catholic Spain. Our painting is a late work of Zurbarán, dating from a time when the elderly artist, abandoning his former austerity, was under the influence of Murillo, the most famous painter of this subject.

68

FRANCISCO DE ZURBARÁN
Fuente de Todos (Estremadura) 1598—Madrid 1664
St. Andrew the Apostle (1630–33)
Oil on canvas, 146.7 × 61 cms.
Inv. no. 50.749
In the Museum since 1950. The painting was at the Alcázar, Seville, until 1810. It was appropriated by Napoleon's Marshal Soult, who sold it in 1835 to the Duke of Sutherland, from whose collection at Stafford House, London, it was auctioned at Christie's on 11 July 1913. It came to Budapest via the art dealer Knoedler & Co., at first in the collection of Ferenc Hatvanyi, later in that of Leopold (Lipó) M. Herzog.

FRANCISCO DE ZURBARÁN
The Immaculate Conception
Oil on canvas, 136.5 × 102.5 cms.
Signed at lower left on the *cartellino*:
Fran(cisc)o De Zurbaran facie(bat) 1661
Inv. no. 800.
From the Esterházy Collection.

P. 70
DIEGO RODRIGUEZ DE SILVA Y
VELÁZQUEZ
Seville 1599—Madrid 1660
Company at Table, or *Peasant Repast* (1619–20)
Oil on canvas, 96 × 112 cms.
Inv. no. 3820.
Formerly in the A. Sanderson Collection,
Edinburgh. Auctioned at Christie's, London, in
1908, when it was bought by Robert Langton
Douglas. Acquired for the Museum the
same year.

VELÁZQUEZ. *Company at Table,* or *Peasant Repast.*

In his early period, in Seville, Velázquez had a liking for so-called *bodegones*—genre subjects enriched by kitchen still-lifes, which were popular in Spain and particularly in Seville, after the example of similarly conceived Dutch paintings, where, however, the figural element gradually disappeared, yielding to pure still-life. Velázquez, who retained his unrelenting truthfulness to nature even when he became a court painter, liked to portray simple, down-to-earth people in their daily life. The same Andalusian peasant, for whom a young woman is here pouring out wine in a glass, can be recognized in *The Repast,* a similar Velázquez painting, in the Leningrad Hermitage, and again as the oldest of the three Magi in the Prado's *Adoration of the Magi.* No less true to the model is the young man at right, shown in pure profile, with his elbows on the table and his right hand raised to underline something he is saying. Velázquez's palette in the Seville period is still limited: except for some touches of white, the old man's bluish-grey clothing, a limited amount of yellow, and some reddish tones the whole painting is dominated by brownish, greyish and blackish tones.

ALONSO CANO. *Noli me tangere.*   *p. 72*

This painting of the resurrected Christ appearing to Mary Magdalen is an evident descendant of Correggio's well-known masterpiece (cf. *Prado/Madrid,* page 26), which Cano saw in the royal collections. The two protagonists are similarly dressed; in this painting, too, the kneeling Magdalen wears a golden black-patterned cloak, and the landscape behind her rises in the same way, while the figure of Christ is again emphasized by a tree. But here Cano has lowered the horizon, Magdalen is auburn-haired, Christ's right hand (pointing up in Correggio's painting) is holding a shovel, and Magdalen is carrying an ointment jar. But what is most important is that the cleft between the two figures in Correggio's painting is now bridged by the movements of Christ's and Magdalen's right hands, so that Correggio's ecstatic meeting has been transformed into a scene of melancholy leave-taking. Cano has changed the subject of *Noli me tangere* into what is, in fact, a version of the well-known, but here somewhat incoherent interpretation of the subject of *Christus tangit Magdalenam.* The whole scene could be hardly understood without the texts of the Gospels (John 20, 14–17, Mark 16, 9), especially because Christ is somehow illogically presented from the viewpoint of Magdalen, who at first thought he was the gardener. The leading authority on Spanish painting, A. L. Mayer, did not hesitate to state that the most essential and noticeable feature of Cano's paintings is their amiable grace.

JUAN CARREÑO DE MIRANDA. *St. James the Greater.*   *p. 73*

The apostle St. James the Greater—whom we have met in this same role of "Moor-Killer" in Tiepolo's painting (cf. page 56)—appears here on a prancing horse. The legendary subject is matched by the picturesque form: in a system of crossing diagonals the victorious rider rises up in strong contrasts of light and shadow. This large canvas was clearly inspired by Pietro Tacca's statue of *Philip IV* on the Plaza de Oriente, Madrid, and

ALONSO CANO
Granada 1601—Granada 1667
Noli me tangere (circa 1646–52)
Oil on canvas, 141.5 × 109.5 cms.
Signed at lower right (on the shovel):
ALO CANO F.
Inv. no. 787.
From the Esterházy Collection. Before 1820 in
the collection of Edmund Burke, London.
Believed to have been originally in the Casita del
Príncipe, Escorial, where it was seen at the end
of the 18th century by Antonio Conca.

follows in the tradition of Leonardo da Vinci's Milanese designs for an equestrian monument. Carreño, a perennial imitator of Rubens, van Dyck and Velázquez, was introduced to the court of Philip IV by the latter. Carreño's great chance came when he replaced his great ideal as leading court painter upon Velázquez's death, and Philip IV was succeeded by his widow Mariana of Austria and their son Charles II. Our painting is one of the artist's weightiest creations, and marks the turning-point between his earlier period—characterized mainly by religious paintings—and his later period, entirely dominated by portraits. To give full justice to the painter—certainly in view of the quality of this picture—we must mention that he occasionally showed, in spite of all the influences so easily absorbed, an independence of mind that even Velázquez often lacked: he refused the knightly Order of Santiago de Espada, which his great predecessor so ostentatiously coveted.

72

JUAN CARREÑO DE MIRANDA
Avilés, Asturia, 1614—Madrid 1685
St. James the Greater
Oil on canvas, 231 × 168 cms.
Signed and dated on the strap on
the horses's breast:
IV CARREÑO F. ANO 1660
Inv. no. 5848.
Gift to the Museum in 1922 from Eugen Boross,
New York. It once hung in the *Galerie
Espagnole* of King Louis Philippe, and was
auctioned at Christie's, London, in 1853.

FRANCISCO DE GOYA Y LUCIENTES. *Portrait of a Lady.*   *p. 75, 76*

Goya's life and work attract, excite and inflame a wide public, far beyond the circle of art amateurs and art experts. He was the last of the versatile old masters of the noble craft of painting, and at the same time the first modernist. In a picture by Goya we at least *know* what we could only *guess at* in earlier painters: whether the task he undertook humanly and artistically engaged him or not. This portrait is believed to represent the wife of his acquaintance Ceán Bermúdez. It certainly belongs to that category of his works in which the painter is attracted not so much by the model, as here by the picturesque dress—the composition of greenish hues, the color relations, the almost impressionistic illusion of transparent and opaque materials, the sparkle of jewelry. Before Goya, the artist remained mindful of the dignity of the sitter, preserving the objective function of portrait-painting to faithfully depict a personality. Now this violent eccentric announces the appearance of a new age, where faithfulness to the model is only one of the many equally important tasks of the painter. The model is left to the mercy—or cruelty—of the creator's vision and judgment, degraded from a personality to a mere person or object.

FRANCISCO DE GOYA Y LUCIENTES
Fuendetodos, Aragon, 1746—Bordeaux 1828
Portrait of a Lady
Oil on canvas, 121 × 84.5 cms.
Inv. no. 3792.
Bought in 1908 from the dealer H. O. Miethke, Vienna. Earlier it was in the collection of the Marquis de Casa Torres, Madrid. The painting is supposed to depict the wife of Juán Augustín Céan Bermúdez, author of a *Diccionario histórico de los más ilustres profesores de las bellas artes en Espana,* published in 1800, which surprisingly does not mention Goya.

FRANCISCO DE GOYA Y LUCIENTES. *The Water-Carrier* and
The Knife-Grinder.   *pp. 77, 78*

Even if Goya's life were not so well documented, his paintings still would tell us a great deal about him. Up to the onset of his illness and deafness in 1792–93 there is little in his painting that transcends the usual frames and leaves the beaten track. It was only then that his eyes opened up, and his great drama began unrolling. Our two comparatively small-sized paintings of Spanish folk characters are for many of us the most precious of all the art treasures preserved in the Budapest Museum: the bright, lively and triumphant *La Aguadora—Water-Carrier—*is a symbol of life-preserving femininity, while her dark male pendant, *El Afilador, The Knife-Grinder,* a low, square-shouldered creature full of terrifying force, is reminiscent of a lurching beast. Both directly confront the onlooker, who stands in the painter's place. The genius who created the *Disasters of War,* the *Third of*

74

May, 1808, and the series of macabre so-called "black paintings" has again and again been considered a bridge between Velázquez and the painter of *Guernica*. But there is some significance in the fact that his life span was closer to Picasso than to Velázquez. On the one hand, there is the world of still intact, self-evident human dignity; on the other, an increasingly endangered, even threatened world shaken to its foundations.

FRANCISCO DE GOYA Y LUCIENTES
The Water-Carrier (1808–10)
Oil on canvas, 68 × 50.5 cms.
Inv. no. 760.
From the Esterházy Collection. Its earlier owner was probably Duke Anton Kaunitz, imperial ambassador in Madrid.

One thing is certain: Goya's depictions of ordinary simple folk—as the two examples above indicate—reveal the artist's sympathetic understanding of the common man. Compared to his official, commissioned portraits, they are marked by highly individualized expression, not only in form, but also in choice of subject matter. Illuminated by penetrating vision, his remarkable powers of characterization and pulsing vitality led him on to tonalities of great intensity, freshness of color and freedom of composition. Like a portentous explosion, this great master suddenly appeared in Spanish painting, and continued to shine with his inborn and imperishable power.

FRANCISCO DE GOYA Y LUCIENTES
The Knife-Grinder (1808–10)
Oil on canvas, 68 × 50.5 cms.
Inv. no. 763.
Same provenance as the preceding painting, with which it is apparently listed together in the inventory of the artist's works from 1812, under no. 13: *Una aguadora y su compañero con el número trece en 300.* The last figure indicates the total value: 300 reals. The paintings have been variously dated: from the painter's very last years in France (A. L. Mayer), or the time before 1820 (Kehrer), to the years around 1805–10 (José López-Rey).

LOW COUNTRIES:
FLANDERS & NETHERLANDS

JAN VAN EYCK. *The Road to Calvary*, 16th-century copy.

From the mighty walls of Jerusalem surrounding a huge central building—the traditional fantasy-image of the Temple—we see a procession with Christ bearing the cross, winding upwards toward the left, between rocks and a crowd of spectators, to Mount Calvary. In front of Christ we recognize the two robbers, with their hands bound on their backs; they are followed by a troop of nobly dressed riders, the first of whom, sitting on a white horse, has been identified by some authorities as the emperor Sigismund, king of Hungary (1363–1437).

Although this is not an original work by Jan van Eyck, but only a fairly faithful copy, the painting is of exceptional importance, for it preserves for us the appearance of a picture probably created in 1422–24, when Jan van Eyck was *valet de chambre* in the court of John of Bavaria at The Hague. The lost original is closely related to several other paintings by the master: *Christ on the Cross between the Virgin Mary and St. John* (Museum Dahlem, Berlin), the two wings with the *Crucifixion* and the *Last Judgment* (cf. *Metropolitan Museum/New York*, page 123), and the well-known seven miniatures that Hulin de Loo has ascribed to the so-called "G. hand," of which four were contained in the Turin Book of Hours, lost by fire in 1904, and the remaining three, *Birth of St. John the Baptist, Mass of the Dead*, and *The Finding of the True Cross*, are today in the Museo Civico, Turin, as a part of the *Milan-Turin Book of Hours*. That is at least how the great majority of experts on early Flemish painting define our painting. A few authors, however, have regarded the Budapest *Road to Calvary* as a copy of some work by Ouwater, and Klára Garas even considers it an original, possibly by Ouwater himself, painted no later than in the fifties of the 15th century.

JAN VAN EYCK
Masseyck (?) circa 1390—Bruges 1441
The Road to Calvary (16th-century copy)
Oil on oak panel, 97.5 × 129.5 cms.
Inv. no. 2531
Acquired in 1904 from the Budapest collection of Ignác Péteri (Pfeffer). Formerly in the collection of the Viennese sculptor Hans Gasser. Sold at auction on 5 April 1869 by Miethke & Wawra.

PETRUS CHRISTUS. *Virgin and Child.*   *p. 83*

JAN VAN EYCK
The Road to Calvary (16th-century copy), detail.

The round arch of a portal, as a kind of majestic frame to the picture, is quite frequent in early Dutch or Flemish altarpieces. Through it we view, on the central axis of this painting, the Virgin with the Child standing on a terrace, along whose marble inlays our eyes move toward the background— the wooden bench covered in the center to seat the two holy personages, beyond which stretches the distant landscape. The Child in the mother's arms, holds up his right hand in a gesture of blessing, and carries in his left a small glass globe surmounted by a cross, symbol of his universal kingship. To indicate the symbolic links between the Old and the New Testaments, the portal shows, in *grisaille*, the sculptures of Adam on the left, and Eve on the right, with a serpent winding around the Tree of Knowledge. The meaning is clear: what the first parents forfeited by their original sin, was redeemed by Christ's incarnation and sacrifice. Eve is juxtaposed with the Virgin, in an iconographical type of representation known in European art since Bernward, the famous bishop of Hildesheim, in the early 11th century, wherein Eve is the *antitypus* of the Virgin, the "new Eve."

Petrus Christus, regarding whose life there are no reliable details except for the place of his birth, the date of his becoming a citizen of Bruges

PETRUS CHRISTUS
Baerle (Brabant) 1415/20—Bruges 1472/73
Virgin and Child (circa 1445)
Oil on oak panel, 55.5 × 31.5 cms.
Inv. no. 4324
The Museum obtained the painting as a legacy
from Count János Pálffy.

82

(1444) and some rough indication of the time of his death, was probably a disciple of Jan van Eyck. Only in this way can we explain the "van-Eyckean" character of his comparatively few known works. Therefore our panel is worthy of special attention: the figure of the Virgin (though not that of the Child) remotely resembles van Eyck's well-known *Madonna at the Well* (Koninklijk Museum voor Schone Kunsten, Antwerp). The paintings of this "artist with an unusual name"—who was apparently also far from insensible to the art of Rogier van der Weyden—are marked by their somewhat simplified but firm plasticity, here shown particularly in the Virgin's face and in the heavy folds of her drapery.

HANS MEMLING
Seligenstadt, circa 1433—Bruges 1494
The Crucifixion
Oil on oak panel, 56 × 63 cms.
Inv. no. 124.
Donated to the National Museum, Budapest, by János László Pyrker in 1836; its previous owner had been Baron Imre(Emerich)Vay, Kécsek. The two wings of which this was the central panel were in the Kunsthistorisches Museum, Vienna; our Museum took them over in 1934, in accordance with the Venice agreement of 1932.

HANS MEMLING. *The Crucifixion.*

Almost a thousand years after the famous *Rabula Gospel* of 586 (Biblioteca Laurenziana, Florence) for the first time depicted the *Crucifixion* as a great dramatic scene with more than a dozen participants, Memling painted his polyptych altarpiece for Lübeck Cathedral (now in the St. Annen-Museum, Lübeck), along with its reduced version, the Budapest triptych, on which experts do not yet agree whether it is a work of the master's own hand or of his workshop. Baldass, together with Friedländer and some others, was of the opinion that it was a workshop product, though at the same time he considered that the smaller altarpiece showed the artist's conception more clearly than the Lübeck polyptych. This central panel of the Budapest *Crucifixion* (and the same applies to the wing scenes) lacks nothing that enlivens the traditional scene. On a hill rising in front of Jerusalem and marked with a skull as Mount Golgotha, under a sky where both the sun and the moon are eclipsed in mourning, we see three crosses, Christ's (*crux commissa*) and the T-shaped ones (*crux immissa*) of the two broken-limbed robbers, of whom the repentant Dismas is turning his face up to the sky, in contrast to the obdurate Gesmas. In the motley crowd we recognize, at left beneath Christ, Longinus transfixing his body with a lance, Stephaton holding out a sponge dipped in vinegar, the group of holy women, among them the swooning Virgin and the hand-wringing Magdalen, and St. John; on the other side, in the crowd of armed men, the centurion revering the Son of God with his raised hand, and in the lower right corner, the soldiers casting dice for Christ's coat. Everything that might be expected is there, but hardly anything we have not seen before—except that in Memling's version the most fatal event of Christian history becomes little more than an efficiently, aptly and fluently staged play.

GERARD DAVID. *The Nativity.*

In his early works, Gerard David—after Memling the last important Bruges master—visibly draws upon the treasures left by his predecessors. The new Western European type of the Virgin "giving birth without pain"—being shown immediately falling on her knees and adoring the newly born Child—had been generally known since the second half of the 14th century. But in our painting the Child lying on the rim of her cloak, and the presence of the two little angels immediately brings to mind the famous *Bladelin Altar* by Rogier van der Weyden (Museum Dahlem, Berlin). As in that painting, the stable is nothing more than a heap of ruins supported by a column that foretells Christ's flagellation, and there is only the burning candle in the shepherd's left hand to tell us that the Son of God was born at night. In the green landscape of the background, which is linked to the foreground by the blossoming bush behind the ruined portal, we can recognize a Flemish city, which here represents Bethlehem; and on a hill at top right the previous event—the *Annunciation to the Shepherds*—is presented simultaneously. The shepherds are supposed to show by their

BAREND VAN ORLEY
Brussels 1488—Brussels 1541
Portrait of Charles V (circa 1516–1519)
Oil on oak panel, 71.5 × 51.5 cms.
Inv. no. 697.
At one time in the Ollingworth-Magniac Collection, London. Bought from the Bourgeois brothers, Cologne, in 1894. One of the workshop replicas is preserved at the Museo e Gallerie Nazionali di Capodimonte, Naples, and two other replicas are in the Louvre.

very postures that they have just arrived: the left one, in a yellow cloak, is already falling to his knees, the younger one behind him—of almost dwarfish proportions—is still standing, while a third one, with black cap, is peering in wonder and curiosity from behind the dilapidated wall of the stable.

JOOS VAN CLEVE. *The Virgin Offering Wine to the Child.*   *p. 86*

The unknown Flemish painter given the provisional name of "Master of the Death of the Virgin," after his altarpieces in the Wallraf-Richartz-Museum, Cologne, and in the Alte Pinakothek, Munich, has been long since identified as Joos van Cleve, a personality deduced by Ludwig Burchard from a somewhat confused report by van Mander. The artist's works, exceeded only by Memling's in extent, show a greater familiarity with Italian painting, especially Leonardo da Vinci. It is not known whether Joos made his acquaintance with Leonardo in Italy itself or in France, where he was, it seems, for some time employed as portrait painter at the court of Francis I. His numerous paintings of graceful, affable Virgins, with more or less recognizable Leonardesque facial traits, are intimate works, intended for private devotion. The curious iconography of this panel, showing the Christ Child drinking from a chalice, continues the tradition of ancient sacred symbols in Madonna and Child paintings from the Low Countries and Italy, such as an apple in the mother's or the child's hands, as a reminder of the original sin and at the same time a symbol of Redemption; or a carnation, signifying the nails of the cross. In this painting the apparently prosaic, genre-like motif of the Child sipping red wine from a glass is, in this context, an allusion to the Last Supper and the miraculous transformation of wine into the saving blood, an event repeated, according to Christian belief, again and again at every celebration of the Mass.

BAREND VAN ORLEY. *Portrait of Charles V.*

Emperor Charles V (1500–1558), in whose world-empire "the sun never sets," was portrayed by many artists, including Bernhard Strigel, Parmigianino, Seisenegger, Amberger, and of course, Titian (cf. *Alte Pinakothek/ Munich*, page 133 and *Prado/Madrid*, page 34). Barend van Orley, court painter to two stadholderesses of the Netherlands—Charles' aunt Margaret of Austria and Charles' sister Mary of Hungary—painted this portrait after the young prince had already become king of Spain (1516). In keeping with an established tradition of Flemish portraiture, he is shown behind a breast-high parapet, on which his left hand is resting. Under a broad-brimmed hat embellished by a precious buckle set with pearls, the head is turned toward the right in a resolute, commanding and ruler-like attitude. We recognize the inherited Habsburg traits—the protruding lower jaw and the heavy lips—and around his shoulders is the wide chain of the Order of the Golden Fleece, founded in 1429 by Philip the Good, Duke of Burgundy. The Habsburgs had inherited that decoration, together with Burgundy in 1477, when Mary, the daughter of Charles the Bold married Maximilian, heir to the imperial throne, Charles' grandfather and immediate predecessor in the Habsburg dynasty.

Far left
GERARD DAVID
Oudewater, circa 1460—Bruges 1523
The Nativity
Oil on oak panel, 76.5 × 56 cms.
Inv. no. 1336.
In the C. J. Nieuwenhuys Collection (auctioned in London in 1886) and in the Spitzer Collection, Paris (auctioned in Paris in 1893). Bought by the Bourgeois brothers, Cologne, in 1894. Another version dating from the same period is in the Cleveland Museum of Art (previously in the Pannwitz Collection); a later and somewhat different version is in The Metropolitan Museum of Art, New York (from the Friedsam Collection).

Left
JOOS VAN CLEVE
(JOSSE VAN DER BEKE)
Antwerp, active from 1511—Antwerp 1540/1541
*The Virgin Offering Wine
to the Child* (circa 1515–20)
Oil on oak panel, 52.5 × 42 cms.
Inv. no. 4329
Obtained as a legacy from Count János Pálffy, who had bought it from the Paris art dealer Charles Sedelmeyer.

JAN SANDERS VAN HEMESSEN. *Isaac Blessing Jacob.*

Hardly anywhere else was the Mannerist quest for the artificial and the unusual so thoroughly fused with undeniable naturalism as in some of the 16th-century painters of the Low Countries. Nowhere are the contrasts between Italian models and an essentially different native tradition so dramatically apparent. These coarse, popular types, all looking *brutti, sporchi e cattivi*, resemble pimps, whores and tramps more than anything else. The violent, agitated figural composition, in a jumble of three-dimensional heads, limbs and bodies with all their deformations and fore-shortenings, is a genuine *tour de force*. The viewer here is at first hardly aware that he is confronted with a Biblical scene, namely the story of the cunning Jacob, who manages by deceit to obtain the blessing of his blind father Isaac, aided by his mother Rebecca. The first-born of the twins, Esau, for whom this blessing was intended, is seen in the far distance on the left, a hairy creature entirely absorbed in his hunting. In other Biblical scenes by Jan Sanders are found the same peculiarities of form, and the same abundance of genre traits, all of which we can justifiably consider the beginnings of Flemish genre painting.

Below
JAN SANDERS VAN HEMESSEN
Hemixen near Antwerp, circa 1500—
Haarlem (?) after 1555
Isaac Blessing Jacob
Oil on oak panel, 119 × 163 cms.
Inv. no. 1049.
Donated to the Museum in 1896 by the Paris art dealer François Kleinberger. A replica is preserved in the Alte Pinakothek, Munich.

PIETER AERTSEN. *Market Scene.*
After Jan van Hemessen, a native of the southern Netherlands, the work of
Pieter Aertsen, a pronounced Northerner, represents the next step toward
the emergence of genre painting as an independent branch, in which
ordinary people amidst their everyday environment and typical activities
are depicted. In contrast to Hemessen's violently interlaced groups, Aertsen's serious-looking, heavy and rigid characters are rather feebly interrelated. The old Dutch peasant with clogs on his feet and a basket with two
ducks in his right hand apparently belongs to the same social class as the
woman behind him, also a market vendor, but we cannot establish any
further relation between them. This stout man with a barrel on his head fills
the full length of the narrow, upright painting, and the archway above him
itself heightens his effectiveness. The painter evidently wished to portray
him in movement, but did not quite succeed. As Friedländer perceptively
put it, Aertsen's chief talent was the depiction of motionless objects, namely
of still-lifes, which in many of his works are, in fact, more prominent than
anything else. Thus he became, in spite of his obvious lack of imagination
and breadth of concept, one of the pioneers in this special iconographic
sphere.

PIETER AERTSEN
Amsterdam, circa 1508—Amsterdam 1575
Market Scene
Oil on oak panel, 170 × 82.8 cms.
Signed with the painter's trademark and dated
1561 on the stone at lower right.
Inv. no. 1337.
Bought from the Bourgeois brothers, Cologne,
in 1894.

Pp. 90–91
PIETER BRUEGHEL THE ELDER
Breda circa 1525—Brussels 1569
Sermon of St. John the Baptist
Oil on wood panel, 95 × 160.5 cms.
Signed and dated: *BRUEGEL M. D. LXVI.*
Inv. no. 512 829.
In the museum since 1951 (bequeathed by Count
Batthyány).

PIETER BRUEGHEL THE ELDER. *Sermon of St. John the Baptist. pp. 90–91*
The wide scene is entirely presented in a sweeping panorama from a single
viewpoint. The central figure of John the Baptist—as often in mannerist art,
and quite particularly in Brueghel's—is almost hidden in the middle of the
immense crowd, although most of those present are turning toward him. It
is even more difficult to find Christ: St. John is pointing to Him, but the
people evidently do not notice Him. In sharp contrast with these two
traditionally represented figures, but here so inconspicuously rendered as to
be somewhat unreal, is the plebeian throng which has been carefully and
realistically characterized. The everyday faces, distinguishable even from
our distant viewpoint, display highly varying degrees of interest and disin-
terest. Brueghel always painted his human figures as types; he knew how to
present their peculiar traits saliently, even if their faces are more or less
hidden, or their backs turned toward the viewer. In the exceptional case
when a figure appears in fashionable dress and with more individual facial
traits, art historians have endeavored to identify it. Terlinden thinks the
man in the foreground whose palm the gypsy is reading represents the
merchant Franckert, a friend of the artist; and de Tolnay sees in the
moustached face above the gypsy, just visible between the backs of two
listeners, a self-portrait of the artist. Previously the *Sermon of St. John* had
been usually only represented in the background of the *Baptism in the
Jordan*. Brueghel and some contemporary Dutch painters—accustomed to
Protestant sermons in the open air!—turned it into the chief subject of the
picture. In our painting the *Baptism in the Jordan* can only be discerned at
a bend of the river winding through the tiny "composite" landscape at
upper right, with a crowd of onlookers watching from the bank.

NICOLAS NEUFCHATEL. *Portrait of Hendrik Pilgram* and
Portrait of Pilgram's Wife.
Our painter, also called *Lucidel,* had to leave his native country because of
his adherence to Calvinism. He is believed to have been in Frisia in the
years before he went to Nuremberg. This could explain why he was
influenced by the only important Frisian artist, the portrait-painter Adriaen
van Cronenburch. The Nuremberg patrician Hendrik Pilgram, or Pelgrom
(1533–1581), born in Hertogenbosch, was painted when he was 28, accord-

ing to the inscription on the picture, while his wife, also a Netherlander, was 11 years younger. The style of the two portraits is clearly neither Dutch nor German, but international. The independent full-length portrait was a type created by both the Italians (Carpaccio, Moretto) and the Germans (Cranach the Elder, Seisenegger). It reached its full bloom in the first great age of the international courtly and aristocratic portrait by painters from every part of Europe, notably Holbein the Younger, François Clouet, Mor, Moroni and Sanchez Coello and others. As in Moroni's portraits, the presentation is here remarkably effective, creating a contrast between the black Spanish costume and the warm incarnadine on the one hand, and the cool, bright pavement and walls on the other.

JAN BRUEGHEL. *The Animals of Noah's Ark.*
The gentle, colorful and calm world of our painting is filled with equally gentle and placid animals. In the background, we see Noah's huge ark, on which the entire company is bound to embark, while behind the trees at right there is a church tower—a somewhat incongruous item in an antediluvian story. Pride of place is given to the horse, clearly imitated from Rubens—a real homage to a friend with whom Jan Brueghel often collaborated. Animals of every kind are shown crowding together in peaceful coexistence, all in couples—one male and one female of each species, as God had commanded to Noah. The underlying principle of this minutely depicted universe is the enumeration of the many attractive curiosities that delight and amuse the eye. The painting is ideally suited for the *cabinets de curiosités,* or *Kunst- und Wunderkammern,* that mark the golden age of European collecting in the transition between the late Renaissance and the Baroque. It was an art for collectors, mostly noblemen and rich burghers,

NICOLAS NEUFCHATEL
(COLYN VAN NIEUCASTEEL)
Mons circa 1527—Nuremberg circa 1590
Portrait of Hendrik Pilgram
Oil on canvas, 180.5 × 94 cms.
Dated at lower left (on pilaster base):
ANNO DOMINI 1561.
Inv. no. 346.
From the Esterházy Collection.

NICOLAS NEUFCHATEL
Portrait of Pilgram's Wife
Oil on canvas, 180 × 94 cms.
Dated at lower left (on pilaster base):
ANNO DOMINI 1561.
From the Esterházy Collection.

JAN BRUEGHEL
Brussels 1568—Antwerp 1625
The Animals of Noah's Ark
Oil on oak panel, 61 × 90, 2 cm.
Inv. no. 548.
From the Esterházy Collection. Replica in the Prado Museum. The original, signed and dated 1615, is in the Duke of Wellington Collection, London.

who had no taste for either deep thoughts, or moralist questionings, but just piled up rare objects, freaks of nature, or smoothly varnished images of a pleasant and agreeable life. Because of his soft, luminous colors Jan was called "Velvet Brueghel."

FRANS FRANCKEN THE YOUNGER. *The Imitation of Christ.*　　　*p. 95*
Frans Francken, second of this name and the most gifted and industrious member of the family, was one of the very few Flemish painters of the time who managed to eschew the influence of Rubens. His amusing paintings, full of tiny details, often depict art collections, for he was—together with "Velvet" Brueghel—the veritable pioneer of "painted galleries," a branch of painting later represented by Teniers, Pannini, Zoffany, and others. In this picture the mode is used to illustrate a devotional allegory, a pictorial presentation of a believer's imitation of Christ, which could hardly be depicted in any other way. At lower right, a woman painter seated before her easel—signifying the Christian soul—has a vision of Christ with an open heart in his hand. To the left behind Christ we see the five Wise Virgins, and deeper in space is shown St. Ann teaching the young Virgin Mary. Near the left edge of the painting, the apprentice mixing colors—familiar from Dutch paintings of artists' studios—is here replaced by two angels, while a few more of these winged creatures are making music in the cloud above. As if in some shop selling Catholic devotional objects, our eyes flicker to and fro between the crucifix, the prayer books, the statues, the many trinkets and the host of pictures and images leaning against the furniture, hanging on the walls and displayed on the table, all on the theme of Christian belief.

PETER PAUL RUBENS (and ANTHONY VAN DYCK).
Mucius Scaevola before Porsenna.　　　*p. 96*
One of the stirring patriotic tales from mythical Roman history tells about the extraordinary heroism of Gaius Mucius. Having failed in his attempt to assassinate the Etruscan king Porsenna who was besieging Rome (he killed the king's scribe by mistake) and being taken prisoner, he lets his right hand burn on an altar to prove his bravery. Both this act and Mucius' assurance that he is only one of three hundred equally fearless conspirators alarm the Etruscan to the point of abandoning his siege and freeing the hero, who was later given the name of *Scaevola*, i.e., Left-Handed. The principal diagonal in the composition—assending from the dead scribe at lower left toward Mucius' right hand and up to the edge of the curtain—divides the whole between a bright half thronged with people and a darker space reserved for Porsenna. Mucius stands intrepidly before the sacrificial altar, his left hand akimbo in a gesture of defiance and triumph, his eyes piercing his adversary, who retreats in revulsion. Rubens' mighty composition, carried out with the help of van Dyck, is by no means exceptional. In the master's thoroughly organized workshop, Rubens often contributed only a color sketch, while some gifted collaborator was entrusted with the production of the full-scale painting, the master himself then returning to retouch special passages.

94

FRANS FRANCKEN THE YOUNGER
Antwerp 1581—Antwerp 1642
The Imitation of Christ
Oil on oak panel, 112 × 148 cm.
Signed at lower right:
Dov. F. Franck fecit.
Inv. no. 53.481.
Formerly collection of Count Ödön Zichy, Vienna; donated by Jenö Zichy to the Museum in 1953.

ANTHONY VAN DYCK. *Portrait of a Man.*

The precocious van Dyck, after Rubens the greatest Flemish 17th-century painter, had the bad luck of being—both in his lifetime and subsequently—always compared with the giant who was almost a generation older, but whom the man perpetually destined to inferior rank survived only by a year and a half. It is known that van Dyck produced independently and had pupils as early as 1615–16, although he did not earn the official title of master until 1618. On the other hand a document from 1620 lists him as one of Rubens' disciples. Although he might be said never to have been literally a pupil of the great master, there is no doubt that he learned a great deal from Rubens, particularly in the sphere of portrait painting, where he best showed his special sensibility, talent and—if we are allowed the expression—obligingness. Among van Dyck's three paintings in the Budapest Museum, this bust-length portrait of an unknown burgher of Antwerp dates from his early, pre-Italian period. The lace collar, painted in impasto technique, clearly shows how close the two painters still were at the time. The painting, once attributed to Rubens, is now definitively considered to be the work of van Dyck.

JACOB JORDAENS. *The Fall of Man.*

Robust, sunburnt and corpulent men and their glamorously fleshy, bulging wives, all of whom seem like countrified and coarsened relatives of Rubens' heroes, not only dominate Jordaens' genre paintings, but also uncouthly invade his mythological and Biblical world. He lived, it must be said, at a time when no Flemish painter could successfully resist the influence of Rubens—least of all when he attempted large-scale "histories." These were precisely Jordaens' favorite subjects, for this painter did not care much about graceful miniatures, and despised portraits in spite of his talents in this field. His Adam and Eve in the present painting are plain, well-fed and palpably sensual beings. The somewhat prosaic choice of animals and plants for a picture of the earthly paradise and such a fatal event—cattle, sheep and pumpkins—is the same in many of his paintings and all constitute, irrespective of the titles and the traditional subjects, one single glorious

JACOB JORDAENS
Antwerp 1593—Antwerp 1678
The Fall of Man
Oil on canvas, 184.5 × 221 cms.
Inv. no. 5551.
Donated to the Museum by Dr. Anton Éber, Dr Oskar Goldfinger and Simon Kraus. The previous owner had been Count Jenö Karátsonyi, Budapest.

hymn to Flemish abundance. Though he was converted to Calvinism in 1645, he apparently suffered no particular difficulties because of this, and he did not hesitate to continue painting altarpieces for Catholic churches till the end of his life.

ADRIAEN BROUWER. *Peasants Smoking.*
More intimately and strongly than any other artist, the eccentric, wild genius Adriaen Brouwer links the two countries of the Netherlands— Flanders and Holland. His paintings created in Amsterdam and Haarlem show evidence of Flemish tradition; but his later works, produced in Antwerp—such as this picture—clearly show that Dutch painting had made the decisive step from local color to integral harmony of tone, subordinating all the figures and interiors to the basic tone of the whole, making them in the process more natural. In short, the artist broke with the

ADRIAEN BROUWER
Oudenaarde (Flanders) 1605/06—Antwerp 1638
Peasants Smoking
Oil on oak panel, 40.7 × 39.3 cms.
Inv. no. 566.
From the Esterházy Collection. A replica (or possibly the original) is in the collection of the Duke of Wellington, Apsley House, London.

tradition of Brueghel's successors, and his genre world thereby became simpler and fresher. With quick brush-strokes and thin applications of paint—the combination of these two traits is Brouwer's specialty—he brings to life his rather vulgar table companions, usually with a restricted number of participants, all coarse, instinct-led beings yielding to their passions and excesses, which here usually means drink and tobacco. The fact that the painter's own life was spent in this sinful world only helped to increase interest in his works. Rubens and other contemporary connoisseurs collected them enthusiastically.

100

FRANS HALS
Antwerp 1580/81—Haarlem 1661
Portrait of a Man (circa 1650)
Oil on oak panel, 64.5 × 46.3 cms.
Inv. no. 277.
From the Esterházy Collection.

FRANS HALS. *Portrait of a Man.* p. 100

Something of the immediacy, exuberance and naturalness of Frans Hals's youthful drinkers, music-makers and merry revelers which has never been matched either in earlier or in later painting, can also be sensed in his portraits. Our painting dates from the period when Hals had definitely abandoned genre subjects and had turned exclusively to portraiture. His former bright colors have yielded to a strongly monochromatic world dominated by black. Hals's great discovery is his slashing impressionistic brush stroke, which allows visual illusion only when viewed from a certain distance, and which—although first employed in his genre paintings—he took over into his commissioned portraits. Not without reason was he admired by French and German Impressionists like Manet and Liebermann. This portrait was listed in the 1812 catalogue of the Esterházy Collection as a self-portrait by Karel Dujardin. It was first ascribed to Hals by Karoly Pulszky, who called it a self-portrait. Later Pigler pronounced it to be a portrait of the well-known landscape painter and Romanist, Jan Asselyn (ca. 1616–1652). Grimm, on the other hand, attributed it to the master's son, Frans Hals the Younger.

PIETER VAN LAER (IL BAMBOCCIO)
Haarlem 1582—Haarlem after 1642
Mora Players, or *The Small Lime-Kiln* (1630)
Oil on oak panel, 33.3 × 47 cms.
Inv. no. 296.
From the Esterházy Collection; at one time probably in the collection of Joachim Sandrart.

PIETER VAN LAER. *Mora Players,* or *The Small Lime-Kiln.*

Van Laer was the central figure of the *Schildersbent,* a brotherhood of Dutch and other Northern painters in Rome. Its members called themselves *bentveughels,* or "flocking birds." Their bohemian lives and the trivial subjects of their paintings brought them into repeated conflicts with the academic artists, purveyors of the "highbrow," official production of religious, mythological and allegorical subjects. Van Laer, called *Il Bam-*

boccio, the Dwarf, because of his sickly, hunchback body, was the first to specialize in genre scenes from the dregs of society. Without any shade of accusation or mockery, he portrayed the real life of the streets and low-down pubs—rustics and beggars, soldiers, tramps and brigands, pedlars and quacks. His range of subjects and his tonalities were imitated by other Northern painters (Jan Miel, Johannes Lingelbach, Michiel Sweerts), and even by some Italians (Michelangelo Cerquozzi). After their master, they were given the contemptuous nickname of *bamboccianti*, and their paintings were called *bamboccciate*. Critics, like Bellori and Passeri, tended to despise them, the only exception being van Laer's friend Joachim von Sandrart; but their works did not lack collectors.

HENDRICK AVERCAMP. *Winter Landscape with Skaters.*
In a flat Dutch landscape, with a farmstead on the left, a windmill and in the far distance, a village with a church tower, we see a host of young and old skaters on a frozen canal. Sailboats and rowboats are frozen in, smoke is cheerfully rising from a chimney, and the birds, forced by cold and hunger to resort to the vicinity of human dwellings, are flying all around the house and alighting on the bare trees. Hendrick Avercamp, deaf-mute from his birth and therefore nicknamed *De Stomme van Kampen* (the Mute of

HENDRICK AVERCAMP
Amsterdam 1585—Kampen 1664
Winter Landscape with Skaters
Oil on oak panel, diameter 30.5 cms.
Signed at left (on the house wall) with an interlaced monogram: *HAV.*
Inv. no. 1698.
Bought in 1899 from the Paris art dealer François Kleinberger. Earlier it had been in the Paris collections of G. Rothan (auctioned in May 1890 at the Gallery Georges Petit) and I. Tabourier (auctioned in June 1898 at the Hôtel Drouot).

Kampen), was the first outstanding Dutch landscape painter of the 17th century, and a real specialist in such pictures. His agreeable paintings show hardly any development. He never got tired of depicting more or less identical scenes over and over again: groups of villagers and visiting towns-folk skating and falling on the ice, sledding, or catching fish. Even the widespread, snow-clad winter landscape itself remains essentially un-changed, enlivened—with slight variations from painting to painting—with the same people, village houses, mills and drawbridges, always under a grey, overcast sky, illumined by a marvelous clear light. It is precisely in this re-creation of the atmosphere that we recognize a typical feature of the new painting of Holland.

CORNELIS VAN POELENBURGH
Utrecht circa 1586—Utrecht, 1667
The Children of the Palatine Elector
Frederic V, King of Bohemia
Oil on oak wood, 37.9 × 65.3 cm.
Signed with monogram at lower right, and dated: 1628.
Inv. no. 381.
From the Esterházy Collection. Previously in the collection of Charles II of England.

CORNELIS VAN POELENBURGH. *The Children of the Palatine Elector Frederic V, King of Bohemia.*

Except for some genre paintings, the most amusing pictures from 17th-century Holland are the portraits showing the good-natured, portly and not particularly refined Dutch burghers in splendid Biblical, mythological or other ancient disguise, anticipating—quite unsuspectingly—Daumier's travesties. Married couples, for instance, might be portrayed as Meleager and Atalanta, appearing in the triumphal scene at the end of the Calydon

103

hunt, where the king's son courteously hands over a boar's head to Atalanta, who had been the first to strike the beast. In our painting by the
Utrecht painter van Poelenburgh, even children are depicted acting in such
a masquerade, although they are in this case of noble birth. In a hilly
landscape seven children are seen posing—they are the offspring of Frederick, the Palatine Elector remembered as the "Winter King" from the

104

NICOLAAS MOEYAERT
Amsterdam 1592/93—Amsterdam 1655
The Cup Found in Benjamin's Sack
Oil on cloth, 94.5 × 138.4 cms.
Signed and dated at lower left:
CL Mooyaart A° 1627.
Inv. no. 1048.
Bought in 1895 from the art dealer C. J. Wawra,
Vienna. The museum also preserves another
painting of the same subject by this painter,
dated 1633.

history of the Thirty Years' War. The eldest, Charles Ludwig, aged about eleven, represents Meleager, while Atalanta is impersonated by his one-year younger sister Elizabeth, seated in the middle. The lance in the hands of one of the brothers, the falcon in the hand of another, and even more the "hunting still-life" with the two dogs at right, show us that the painter has combined a children's group portrait with a mythological scene and a real hunting picture. The elder of the two boys draped in classical costume—the one closest to Elizabeth—is Prince Rupert, born in 1619, who later became Palatine Elector, Royalist leader in the English civil war and an English admiral in the war against the Netherlands. He also left an important mark in the annals of art history: he was one of the pioneers of a new technique of graphic art, the *mezzotint*.

NICOLAAS MOEYAERT. *The Cup Found in Benjamin's Sack.*
Jacob's son Joseph, who had become a mighty ruler in Egypt, once again put to test his brothers who had come to him for food without recognizing him. Joseph ordered his silver cup to be surreptitiously hidden in the sack of the youngest, Benjamin, and then sent a steward after them to "find" the precious object. "And he searched, beginning with the eldest and ending with the youngest; and the cup was found in Benjamin's sack." The turbaned rider at left represents the steward; and at right are the eleven stunned, frightened, and despairing brothers, among them the little Benjamin, weeping, with the hand of a helmeted soldier on his shoulder—a gesture that helps to link the two unequal groups. Moeyaert was, like Rembrandt's teacher Pieter Lastman, educated in Rome under the influence of Elsheimer. Like Lastman, Moeyaert portrayed large groups of people excitedly reacting to some dramatic event. No doubt, we find ourselves here in that same narrative world marked by *chiaroscuro*, out of which Rembrandt's painting also developed. Art historians have observed that the animals in Moeyaert's paintings are no less carefully depicted than his human characters, which has led some of them to conclude that he was a teacher of the animal painter Paulus Potter. It is known that among Moeyaert's followers were Nicolaes Berchem and Jan Baptist Weenix, two landscape painters who were both also important portrayers of animals.

JAN VAN GOYEN. *Seascape with Fishermen.* *p. 106*
We can almost physically sense the humid fragrance of the air, the quiet sea, and the enormous sky covered with low-hanging rain clouds above the unusually low horizon. In the foreground we see the dark figures of fishermen in their boats and sea gulls flying low above the water; then, as our eyes glide toward the far distance, everything becomes increasingly flooded with light. Jan van Goyen, an eminent painter and draughtsman, was taught by five different masters successively, but was profoundly influenced only by the sixth, Esaias van de Velde, of Haarlem. Once he had become really independent, his painting turned almost monochromatic, with prevailing brownish-yellow and greyish-green tones, which allowed him to emerge in the 1630s as the leading master of "tonal" landscape

painting in his country. The subjects he introduced were henceforth destined to dominate: river landscapes, marines and seascapes such as this painting, images of wide spaces, of atmosphere, of light and of water, to which the new technique of gentle brush strokes applied "wet on wet" is perfectly adapted. Van Goyen was unable to earn enough by the sales of his paintings and was in perpetual financial difficulties.

PIETER SAENREDAM. *Interior of the Nieuwe Kerk, Haarlem.*
No Dutch artist of the 17th century reproduced the monuments of architecture so carefully, so faithfully, and so poetically, as the hunchback recluse Pieter Saenredam, the "first portrait-painter of architecture." He was a perfectionist, who always conscientiously (one could say, with all the methodicalness of a professional, and with all the enthusiasm of an amateur) tells us in great detail in his notes whenever he alters the smallest feature of what he actually saw *in situ*. The major part of his work consists of church exteriors and interiors, presented from an extended field of vision. Usually he produced them in three phases. The first was a careful sketch, followed by a second, more detailed sketch, founded on measures and ground-plans; only later, sometimes several years afterwards, the artist developed his oil painting on a wood panel. Here we see the interior of the Church of St. Ann, the so-called *Nieuwe Kerk*, Haarlem, which he portrayed several times and where he is buried—a painting that can serve as an example of his many others. We notice an austere, bare, whitewashed Calvinist church interior, which contains, in addition to a few tombstones and coats-of-arms, hardly anything but the unavoidable pulpit, chandeliers

and benches, and a few tiny human figures which serve only to indicate the scale. The whole architectural framework, with all its supporting and articulated members, the entire building from the inlaid pavement to the ribbed vaulting, rises before our eyes, clear, bright and immaculate—like a poem of pure reason.

PIETER CLAESZ. *Still-Life with Pastry and Wine-Glass.*
With Pieter Claesz and Willem Heda, Dutch still-life painting reaches its maturity in a synthesis of harmonious tones. The painting often presents a cloth-covered table on which the remains of a delicious meal are left piled up, while some curvilinear slice of fruit usually serves as *repoussoir*, as a

means of giving depth to the painting and spatially separating it from—and linking it to—the viewer. Pieter Claesz is, on the whole, simpler and more modest in his choice of subject matter than the slightly older Heda. In this painting all the objects are arranged along a diagonal, which descends, following the light, from upper left to lower right, with the symbolical vine and wine-glass at one end, and the bread at the other. The wine is half-drunk, the pastry shows the signs of voracious inroads, the walnuts are cracked, the bread is broken. At first sight it seems simply as if somebody had just left the table. Then we begin to wonder if there is not, after all, some deeper meaning. And indeed, not only the more or less official *Vanitas* still-lifes, but also the pictures of "left-overs" convey the idea of the transience of all enjoyments. But even this interpretation can be contradicted: our delight at a deceptively illusionistic reproduction of palpable reality is only heightened by the sad foreboding of transitoriness, and life becomes even more precious and worth living.

PIETER CLAESZ
Burgsteinfurt (Westphalia) 1597/98—
Haarlem 1660
Still-Life with Pastry and Wine-Glass
Oil on oak panel, 63.6 × 88.3 cms.
Signed (on the blade of the knife) with monogram *PC*, and dated 1647.
Inv. no. 1026.
Bought in 1889 at H. O. Miethke's, Vienna.

SALOMON VAN RUYSDAEL. *After the Rain.*   p. 110

We do not know the names of Salomon's teachers, but his chief early influences were certainly Esaias van de Velde and Pieter de Molijn. As many of his paintings are dated, his development is not difficult to trace. For some time his river landscapes and his seascapes resembled those of van Goyen, while his later pictures show a strengthening of the composition, under the evident influence of his nephew's dramatic landscapes. Our museum possesses no less than nine of his pictures, and this one, the earliest of all, well illustrates his own, de Molijn's and van Goyen's "new Haarlem style of landscape-painting," in which the emphasis has definitely shifted from human figures to the landscape itself. The air looks washed-out, lit by the changing light flickering from behind the rushing storm clouds, and set off against the soft sandy ground and the glittering gravel path leading toward the village. At its edge, in front of the house, half-hidden behind the precisely drawn foliage of the trees, a fully loaded cart is waiting. At right, in the shadow under the tree, we discern the dark silhouette of a rider; and on the left we see a lone little hand-cart and a few barrels lying around. That is all—and we look in vain for any trace of anecdote. The critic Max J. Friedländer, who always finds the right word at the right time, observed that in van Goyen's paintings the weather always looks as if it was just about to rain, while in Ruysdael's pictures we feel that the rain is over, and a fresh wind has just dispersed the rain-clouds.

REMBRANDT VAN RIJN. *The Old Rabbi.*

This painting was created when the then roughly thirty-six-year-old Rembrandt was finishing his celebrated *Night Watch*, the year of Saskia's death. But while the *Night Watch* is the triumphant finale of his baroque period, the *Old Rabbi* already belongs to his more intimate painting of the 1640s, when Rembrandt was quite particularly devoting himself to graphic art. Yet figures of wise, solitary, abandoned old people, sunk in their impenetrable reveries, accompanied the artist throughout his career. Often these are figures of saints or other biblical personalities, but in many cases they are simply portraits or generalized studies of the artist's relatives and acquaintances, or—last but not least—his Jewish neighbors and friends. In the spiritualized, deeply humanist mind of the great master—who at that time, and for a long time afterwards, lived on the *Jodenbreestraat* of Amsterdam's Jewish quarter—both the world of the Bible and of his own contemporaries, are more intimately fused than ever before in the European West, sometimes so completely that we can hardly distinguish which is which.

Below
SALOMON VAN RUYSDAEL
Naarden (Gooiland) 1600/03—Haarlem 1670
After the Rain
Oil on oak panel, 56 × 86.5 cms.
Signed with monogram and dated at lower right:
SvR 1631.
From the Esterházy Collection.

REMBRANDT VAN RIJN
Leiden 1606—Amsterdam 1669
The Old Rabbi
Oil on oak panel, 70.5 × 53.5 cms.
Signed and dated at lower left:
Rembrandt f. 1642.
Inv. no. 235.
From the Esterházy Collection.

JAN LIEVENS. *Petrus Egidius de Morrion.*

The inscription beneath the oval picture identifies the date, the name of the man portrayed, and his unusually advanced age of 116 years. Lievens' painting shows an arrangement frequently met in the Baroque period: an illusionistically depicted stone frame around the portrait, a device apparently borrowed from 16th- and 17th-century graphic art, which was the first to use it around engraved portraits. Surrounded by this "inner frame" the contrast between the flesh tones of the portrait and the monochromatic cartouche only helps to heighten the deceptive appearance of a true-to-life presence. Jan Lievens, the precocious Leiden friend of the one-year-older

JAN LIEVENS
Leiden 1607—Amsterdam 1674
Petrus Egidius de Morrion
Oil on oak panel, 83.5 × 59 cms.
Dated: *Aº 1637*
Inv. no. 4311.
Legacy from Count János Pálffy, who bought the painting in 1860 from the Bourgeois brothers, Cologne.

Rembrandt, shared his workshop with him until the latter moved to Amsterdam. While they had collaborated closely and influenced one another in Leiden, they took entirely different paths later on. Lievens, after some three years in England, settled in Antwerp, where he took to imitating Rubens and in particular van Dyck, with such success that some authorities have considered our painting to be the work of van Dyck.

ADRIAEN VAN OSTADE. *Man Sharpening a Pen.*
Ostade's early paintings—of caricatured, rough, uncouth rustics brawling and reveling in miserable country pubs—were evidently inspired by Adriaen Brouwer, when he was apprenticed to Frans Hals. But in his following period Ostade's human figures are much more natural and individualized. The entire painting is harmonized, all bathed in a warm brown Rembrandtesque twilight. It is to this period that we can ascribe this small,

113

apparently modest, but exquisite picture of a man seriously absorbed in his negligible, though demanding task. It shows us how little subject matter is actually needed to create a masterpiece of genre painting. Aside from the figure we can hardly distinguish anything else: some trinkets on the mantel shelf, and an open book and an inkpot on a corner of the table. All the action is concentrated on watching: the man's eyes, glimmering through the heavy lids, are directed parallel to the falling diagonal of the painting. If our man belonged to a series of the Five Senses, he would certainly represent Sight.

AELBERT CUYP. *Cows at a Watering Place.* *p. 114*

We are probably somewhere at the mouth of the Maas River, in the countryside that gave Cuyp his favorite motifs. In the foreground are some grazing cows, with their legs reflected in the shallow water and their heads standing out against the bright horizon; far beyond, on the further bank, we see a church and, on the right, several sailboats, while the whole is interlinked by the golden light of a late afternoon, a device which our painter, who probably never visited Italy, had taken over from Jan Both. Cuyp, a distinguished and well-to-do citizen of Dordrecht whom all the sources in the town's archives simply refer to as "proprietor," also devoted himself to etchings, like many other contemporary Dutch painters. As a painter he created masterfully both big and small pictures, including landscapes, animals and portraits, persistently combining all these three subjects. His portraits of riders set in a landscape, for instance, anticipate English 18th-century painting.

AELBERT CUYP
Dordrecht 1620—Dordrecht 1691
Cows at a Watering Place
Oil on oak panel, 59 × 74 cms.
Signed at lower left: *A. cuÿp.*
Inv. no. 408.
From the Esterházy Collection; earlier in private
English ownership.

JAN STEEN. *The Cat Family.* *p. 116, 117*

Steen's paintings never bore us. They usually stage noisy, merry companies, in which the painter himself and his family often appear. But in this highly natural and carefree life, we can often trace echoes of traditional iconography, and even find some moral lessons, which may not always seem entirely convincing, but can in no way be overlooked. In his paintings all five senses find abundant nourishment, and our present masterpiece might well even literally represent this ancient subject. The seated man holding a sheet of paper—which is a self-portrait of the artist—and the woman leaning on his shoulder and looking down at him, identified as a daughter of van Goyen, both evidently stand for Sight. The girls with the soft-haired cats signify Touch; the bumpkin sipping wine in left foreground and the wiser raven below, who only dares to sniff the wine, stand for Taste and Smell; and all the music-making and shouting, fiddling, piping, barking and mewing, represents Hearing. On longer inspection of the picture, we find that more or less everyone is active with all his or her senses. But the moral lesson is not far away: as noise is followed by silence and joy by sadness, so the enjoyment of life leads to death. The kind painter has apparently reserved this lesson for himself: he has tactfully placed the skull above his own head.

JACOB VAN RUISDAEL. *View of Amsterdam.*   *p. 119*
In Jacob van Ruisdael's work Dutch landscape painting achieved its synthesis and climax. In his mighty *oeuvre* we find both sandbank landscapes and seascapes, scenes reminiscent of Philips de Koninck's wide panoramas, views of cities and of marshy woods, winter scenes now turned somber and without the merry skaters, and even—rather unusual for Holland—swift mountain torrents, rapids and waterfalls, i.e., subjects taken over from Allaert van Everdingen, who had brought them from Sweden. But what distinguishes Ruisdael most from either the older or the contemporary landscape painters are his dramatically transformed wholes, his emotional intensity—often tinged with a feeling of melancholy—and his firm monu-

117

mentality and tectonics, so completely different from the cheerfully peopled and building-strewn "ideal landscapes" of the European South. The trees, dead or alive, the mills and the castles are the real heroes of his increasingly subjective universe, which seems to be one single fatal interaction between birth and death. This painting, showing the river Amstel in the foreground and the belfry of the Zuiderkerk in the background, is one of the artist's characteristic mature works. The coexistence of warm and cool tones and the intimate fusion of natural and man-transformed elements masterfully establish an inseparable link between earth and sky, with masses of clouds mirrored in the sunlit and shadowy world below.

JACOB VAN RUISDAEL
Haarlem 1628/29—Amsterdam (?) 1682
View of Amsterdam
Oil on canvas, 52.5 × 43.5 cms.
Signed at lower right with the monogram *VR*.
Inv. no. 4278.
Legacy from Count János Pálffy. One of the earlier owners was Duke Paul Demidoff at San Donato near Florence.

PIETER DE HOOCH. *Woman Reading a Letter.*   *p. 120*
The clean, cultivated interiors in Dutch paintings have a marvelously soothing effect. Through the open window—allowing a glimpse of greenery, red roofs, and the Westerkerk belfry of Amsterdam—the light floods in from the right. The early afternoon sun gently illumines the young woman completely absorbed in the letter she is holding to the light with both hands. Soft shadows glide along the walls, the carefully scrubbed floorboards and the oriental rug covering the table. In deep shade or emerging in light can be seen a decorated leather chair, an open book on the table, a half-drawn curtain, and two paintings—one in a gilt frame at upper left, of which only a lower corner is visible, and a dark one on the right. In this inviolate burghers' intimacy there is nothing to disturb the eye—we can literally feel the silence reigning not just in this room, but also in the world outside. De Hooch's characters seem always naturally engaged in their everyday occupations, entirely unaware of any onlooker. In this painting the artist is at the summit of his development, achieved in Delft and in his early Amsterdam years, when he devoted himself almost exclusively to painting interiors.

ANONYMOUS DUTCH PAINTER. *Portrait of a Woman.*   *p. 121*
This Dutch burgher's wife will probably retain the secret of her identity for a long time to come. The portrait unquestionably dates from the middle of the 17th century. This is indicated, for example, by the dress, which closely resembles that worn by the wife of Willem van der Helm in the *Family Portrait* painted in 1655 by Barent Fabritius (Rijksmuseum, Amsterdam).

But the name of the personage portrayed in this superb painting remains unknown, as well as its author. In the 19th century it was—with a greater or smaller degree of certainty—considered to be the work of Rembrandt; then the picture was for a long time regarded as a Vermeer masterpiece— from Frimml down to Bode and Valentiner, until the time of the notorious van Meegeren forgery affair, when Vermeer's opus was generally reduced to its present more restricted extent. Now the attribution has reverted, if not to Rembrandt himself, at least to his circle. A technical examination has supported this thesis, up to a point. It has been established that the picture is grounded by three layers of paint, first with a layer of red, then one of grey, and finally one of black. This procedure is unknown in any of Vermeer's undoubted creations, but it is frequent in the work of the young Rembrandt and in the paintings from his entourage.

PIETER DE HOOCH
Rotterdam 1629—Amsterdam (?) after 1683
Woman Reading a Letter
Oil on canvas, 55 × 55 cms.
Signed at lower right, and dated 1664.
Bought in 1923 from a private Budapest owner.
Previously in the collection of Count Esterházy at Pápa.

Facing page
ANONYMOUS DUTCH PAINTER
Portrait of a Woman
Oil on canvas, 82 × 65 cms.
Inv. no. 316.
From the Esterházy Collection.

JAN VAN DER HEYDEN. *Interior with Curiosities.*

Van der Heyden's best-known works are views of Amsterdam and other cities, for which he was called "the Dutch Canaletto." In later years he also painted still-lifes, and the inscription on this example tells us that it was painted when he was 75 years old. In this diminutive burghers' version of the traditional ducal *chambres de merveilles* we find an association of objects representing art and science, history, geography, biology, astronomy and astrology. The picture above the marble fireplace represents *The Death of Dido*, after the painting by Antonio Testa, copied by van der Heyden from a print. To the right in front of an ebony cabinet for rare objects are a geographical globe, several spears and two open books; and a stuffed lobster is hanging in front of the painting. The artist, whose city views continued to be imitated for a long time also left his mark in Amsterdam history as an inventor and administrator—he improved the city's lighting system, invented a fire engine for the local fire brigade, and became a rich man.

122

JAN VAN DER HEYDEN
Gorinchen (Gorkum) 1637—Amsterdam 1712
Interior with Curiosities, (1712)
Oil on canvas, 75 × 63.5 cms.
Signed at right (on the chair): *J.v.d.H. 75 Jar.*
Inv. no. 201.
From the Esterházy Collection. In 1776–1813 recorded in various private Amsterdam collections.

CENTRAL EUROPE:
GERMANY
AUSTRIA

HANS HOLBEIN THE ELDER. *Death of the Virgin.*　　*Below and detail right*

The Virgin, in a fashionable headdress, young and beautiful even at the time of her death, is reclining on a canopy bed surrounded by the apostles, all in the ample folds of late-Gothic drapery. St. John leaning over on left side of the bed is holding the palm of martyrdom in his right hand and respectfully offering a candle to the Virgin with his left; St. Peter, standing behind him with an open book, is sprinkling holy water on the dying woman; St. Philip, at extreme left, recognizable by his tall cross-staff, has stopped in trepidation on entering the room. In a cloud above are two angels with censers and between them is the soul of the Virgin, in the traditional representation of her as a small girl received by Christ. This painting shows how even in his earliest works, the elder Holbein introduced highly realistic details in conventional religious themes—seen here in the treatment of the setting, and in particular in the highly individualized faces. This tendency typifies the distinctive talents of the Holbein family in the field of portraiture, and of Holbein the Elder in particular, as demonstrated by about 150 known portrait drawings by him.

Left and detail right
HANS HOLBEIN THE ELDER
Augsburg circa 1465—Isenheim 1524
Death of the Virgin (circa 1485–90)
Oil on oak panel, 150 × 228.5 cms.
Signed and dated on the container of holy water
(the last two figures of the date are illegible).
Inv. no. 4086.
The painting is believed to have been intended
for the tomb of the Preu family in St. James's
Church, Straubing. Later it was in private
ownership in Augsburg and Austria. In 1911 it
was donated to the Museum by the art dealer F.
Kleinberger.

ALBRECHT DÜRER (?). *Portrait of a Man.*   *p. 126*

An almost insoluble problem of attribution is posed by this lyrically soft portrait of a young man dressed in a dark suit and wearing a netted cap, against a vivid red background—one of those flat, monochromatic backgrounds typical of early 16th-century German painting, here objectified only by the shadow of the head. From Tausing down to Winkler and Panofsky, all the authorities on Dürer's paintings included it, without the slightest reservation, as his work. Stadler was the first to ascribe the painting—with a question mark—to Hans Süss, called Kulmbach. This attribution was later strongly supported by Holzing, and finally accepted also by Panofsky, who however believed the man portrayed to be Dürer's twelve-years-younger brother, the goldsmith Andreas Dürer. Nevertheless, the painting can in no way be convincingly included among Kulmbach's early works; and another attribution was suggested by Oetinger, who called it the work of a still more famous follower of Dürer, Hans Baldung. The original attribution to Dürer was seriously weakened when it was found that the blurred outlines cannot be explained as the result of restorations and cleanings—in other words, that the painting has lacked Düreresque sharpness and precision from the very beginning.

Pp. 128–129
LUCAS CRANACH THE ELDER
Kronach, Upper Franconia, 1472—Weimar 1553
Christ and the Adulteress
Oil on linden panel, 82.5 × 121 cms.
Signed with the trademark of Cranach's
workshop and dated 1532.
Inv. no. 146.
From the Esterházy Collection.

ALBRECHT DÜRER
Nuremberg 1471—Nuremberg 1528
Portrait of a Man (early 16th century)
Oil on fir panel, 43 × 29 cms; painted surface
40.4 × 28.2 cms.
Inv. no. 142.
As part of the collection of the Dutch
stadholder, Archduke Leopold William, the
painting was brought from Brussels to Vienna,
whence it was transferred first to Bratislava,
then to Buda Castle, and in 1848 to the National
Museum, Budapest.

LUCAS CRANACH THE ELDER. *Christ and the Adulteress.*   *pp. 128–129*

This well-known and frequently quoted Gospel story (John 8, 3–11), was depicted some fifteen times by Cranach and his workshop. The woman caught *in flagrante*, whom the scribes and Pharisees brought to Christ, was absolved by Him. Christ's words proclaiming that whoever of those present was free of sin should throw the first stone at her, are quoted in the inscription at top center: *WER VNDER EVCH AN SVND IST DER WERFE DEN ERSTEN STEIN AVEF SI.* In the flat decorativeness of this painting, with its flowing outlines and smooth, polished surfaces, the accusers are set against the uniform dark background in vivid contrast to the radiant young sinner and her defender. The scribes on either side are portrayed in accordance with the Gospel story—the oldest being the ugliest, for they carry the most sins on their conscience. While they are predominantly caricatures, and Christ is presented as a simple, sweet figure, the adulteress, with her eyes lowered in shame, is certainly the most lifelike, showing the painter's recurrent type of feminimity, shrewd and never too conscience-stricken.

127

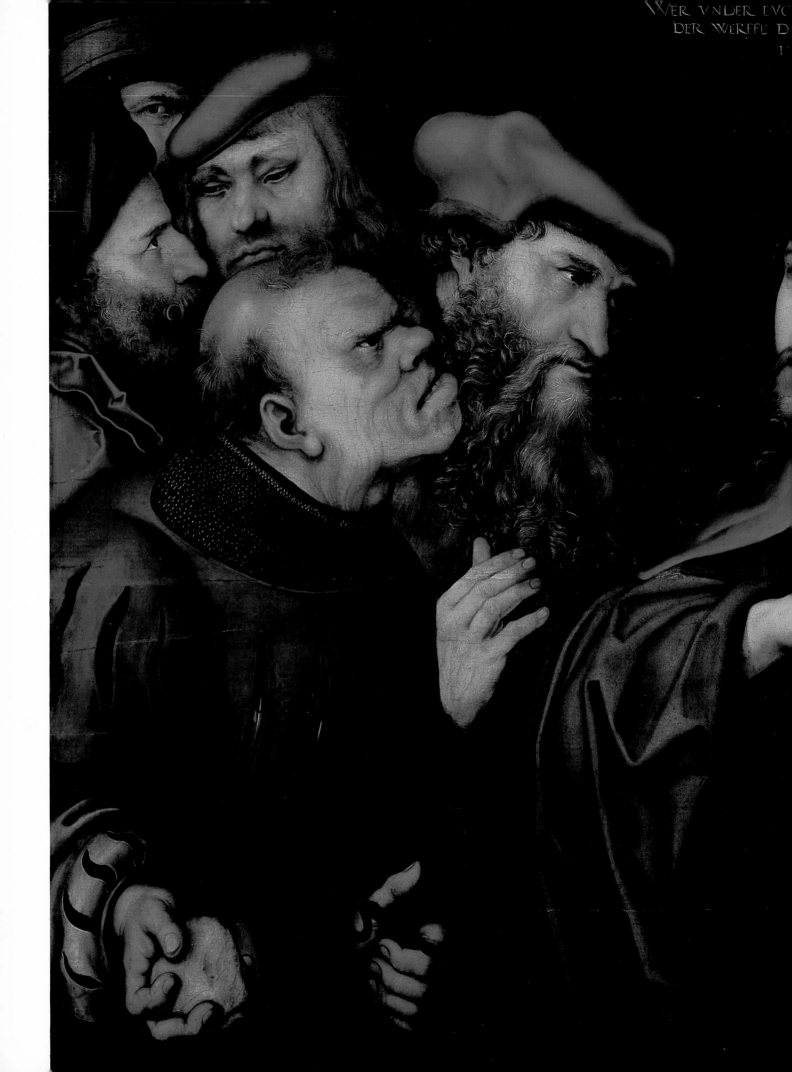

WER VNDER EVC
DER WERFFE D
I

LUCAS CRANACH THE ELDER. *Salome.*

Cranach was a friend of Luther, court painter to three prince-electors of Saxony, and thrice mayor of Wittenberg. He soon became one of the richest citizens of the town, for in addition to his large painter's workshop, he also successfully managed his own printing house and bookshop. As publisher, he emerged as the central figure of the new Protestant art of illustration, even though he at the same time continued to work for the Catholic Church. In addition to biblical and Gospel subjects he painted mythological

LUCAS CRANACH THE ELDER
Kronach, Upper Franconia, 1472—
Weimar 1553
Salome (circa 1530)
Oil on poplar panel, 87 × 58 cms.
Inv. no. 132.
From the Esterházy Collection.

scenes, and last but not least, his frankly sensual female nudes, which aroused Picasso's interest four hundred years later. Among his particularly successful figures are his dissolute courtesans depicted under the guise of the two celebrated *"kephalophores"* of the female sex, the virtuous Judith and the sinful Salome, who can hardly be identified by anything except their traditional attributes—Judith's sword and Salome's plate. Our white-skinned and blue-eyed beauty, sumptuously adorned and carrying her dreadful attribute, is a close relative of the numerous other Salomes and Judiths by Cranach.

ALBRECHT ALTDORFER. *The Crucifixion.*
Not only in its gold background—which is certainly unusual for the

ALBRECHT ALTDORFER
Regensburg or Amberg, circa 1478—
Regensburg 1538
The Crucifixion (circa 1520–25)
Oil on linden panel, 75 × 57.5 cms.
Signed at lower right with the artist's
monogram.
Inv. no. 5892.
Acquired in 1922 from the Countess Erdödy *née*
Irma Mingazzi. One of the earlier owners was
Cardinal Christoph Mingazzi. Prior to that it
was at the monastery of Augustinian canons, St.
Florian, Upper Austria.

131

ascribed date of this work, perhaps because of a whim of the patron—but also in many of its other aspects, this *Crucifixion* is full of irrationality and fancy. The shrill, sharply contrasting colors of this "genuine, spontaneously grown, earth-linked" German painter almost make us overlook the many traits he took from the Italian masters. In this composition, the group of women busy around the swooning Virgin is copied from Mantegna's etching, *Descent from the Cross*, and the red-hued St. John from another print from the same workshop, *Christ's Burial*. But even though all the space is filled with a dense throng of people and horses—among which only Christ on the cross, and the angels stand out—this painting makes us remember that Altdorfer was always more attracted to landscape than to man. Both south and north of the Alps, this was a time when a synthesis of man and landscape was first achieved. Wild nature—immense, untamed and full of animal force—somehow manages to draw all human life and existence into its orbit. The throng on Mount Calvary looks like a thicket, exuberantly spreading, growing and interweaving, in spite of all the well-drawn details difficult to follow, and in spite of the familiar subject frighteningly imponderable and incomprehensible.

HANS BALDUNG, called GRIEN
Schwäbisch-Gmünd 1484/85—Strasbourg 1545
Adam and *Eve* (circa 1525)
Oil on linden wood, each panel 208 × 83.5 cms.
Inv. no. 1888 (Adam) and 1889 (Eve).
Bought in 1900 from the Vienna art dealer D.
Artaria & Co. Prior to that in the collection of
the Counts Schönborn-Buchheim.

HANS BALDUNG, called GRIEN. *Adam* and *Eve*.   *p. 133*
The couple of our first parents at the Budapest Museum was once combined with two full-length nudes against a black background, a *Judith*, dated 1525 (Germanisches Nationalmuseum, Nuremberg), and a *Venus with Cupid*, dated twice, 1524 and 1525 (Rijksmuseum Kröller-Müller, Otterlo). That these four panels belonged together is proved not merely by their style and dimensions, but also by a manuscript preserved at the University Library, Basel, *Humanae industriae monumenta* by Remigius Faesch, who mentions that four such life-size nudes by Baldung were sent in 1641 from Strasbourg to a merchant in Basel. Among the masters of the German Renaissance not even Cranach expressed his erotic fancies so unrestrainedly as this gifted follower of Dürer. Baldung painted altarpieces, allegories and portraits, made woodcuts and designed stained-glass windows. But his special contribution to Renaissance art lies in his numerous drawings, which possess a value as independent works of art—as do those of Dürer and Holbein. When observing our two paintings—the exuberant posture of the dark, muscular, faun-bearded, strutting peacock-like *Adam*, and the contrasting pose of the coquettish, seductive, fair-haired *Eve*—we realize at once that we are far in the artist's classical period, following closely on the painter's voluptuous *Two Witches* (Städelsches Kunstinstitut, Frankfurt). In Baldung's work, profane subjects played an important part from the very beginning.

132

Left
JOHANN LISS
Oldenburg region, north of Lübeck, circa 1597—
Venice circa 1630
Judith with the Head of Holofernes (1620)
Oil on canvas, 129 × 104 cms.
Inv. no. 4913.
Donated to the Museum in 1916 by Dr. Ernst
Kammerer. Probably at one time owned by the
Vidiman family, Venice.

JOHANN LISS. *Judith with the Head of Holofernes.*

The Israelite heroine, the beautiful widow of Manasseh, beheaded the Assyrian commander Holofernes with his own sword, thereby saving her people during the siege of Bethulia. Liss, a North-German who had settled in Italy, brilliantly combined the impulses from Flemish and from Roman painting, in balanced composition and Baroque violence. Almost the entire canvas is filled with the mighty figures of the somewhat vulgarly sensual young woman and the beheaded Assyrian, from whose neck the blood can be seen spurting. Everything else takes second place. Liss apparently managed to provoke quite a sensation with this blood-curdling picture.

SALOMON ADLER. *Self-Portrait.* *p. 135*

In this unusual self-portrait, *Salomone di Danzica* appears to have portrayed himself twice. We see him first of all as he looked when the picture was painted, i.e., some time in the 1680s; and secondly, as he was in his youth, let us say, when he had just arrived in Italy from the north. The

SALOMON ADLER
Gdańsk (Danzig) 1630—Milan (?) 1691 or later
Self-Portrait
Oil on canvas, 128 × 98 cms.
Inv. no. 1896.
Bought in 1901 from the estate of Pál Almássy,
Budapest.

utter contrast between the serious-looking and distrustful young man in neat dark clothing, and the affable, broadly smiling and somehow homely old painter in the bright satin suit, is evidently deliberate. It appears to be patterned on the famous contrasting pair of the "laughing" and "weeping" philosophers, Democritus and Heraclitus—a highly popular theme in the 17th century. Salomon Adler had probably been a pupil of Daniel Schultz in his native Danzig, while his own best-known disciple was the portrait painter Vittore Ghislandi. His surviving works include a few portraits of Lombardian and Venetian aristocracy, and roughly the same number of self-portraits. Our Budapest self-portrait is a practically unaltered replica, very probably by the painter's own hand, of the version preserved in the Uffizi Gallery, Florence. The double portrayal of the painter in early and late years is by no means entirely unprecedented. The Dutchman David Bailly and the Florentine Carlo Dolci had used the same idea before, though in an entirely different way.

Facing page
JOHANN ZICK
Lachen near Ottobeuren 1702—Würzburg 1762
Gad the Prophet in the Presence
of David (circa 1750–60)
Oil on canvas, 48 × 35 cms.
Signed at lower right: *Jo. Zick inv. et pinx.*
Inv. no. 6510.
On permanent loan from the Society of Friends
of the Art Museum (since 1932).

JOHANN ZICK. *Gad the Prophet in the Presence of David.*   *p. 137*
In addition to the many 18th-century fads—Chinese, Russian, and Turkish—there was also a rage for Rembrandt, which was apt not only to simplify, but actually to distort the image of the great artist. The most cursory glance at the figures and the peculiar play of light and shade in this picture reveals that the painter imitated Rembrandt in trying to present a biblical scene. The king sitting on the canopied throne is David (with the harp, attribute of the psalmist, leaning on the chair at his side); the old man facing him was once considered to be Nathan, but after J. Nieuwstraten's convincing explanation there can be no doubt he represents Gad the Seer, who had come to David on God's command, to give him the choice of three punishments (2 Samuel 24, 13): "Should three years of famine come over your country? Or should you flee for three months from the enemies pursuing you? Or should your country be stricken with a pestilence for three days? Think now, and decide what I am to reply to him who has sent me!" The angel hovering above Gad is holding the symbols of the three punishments: a bundle of rods, for famine; a sword, for flight from adversaries; and a skull, for pestilence. Though the influence of Rembrandt reached the Bavarian court painter in devious ways, chiefly through his prints, it can also be felt in the very method of painting.

JANUARIUS ZICK. *Elisha and the Sunammite Boy.*

The prophet Elisha, successor to Elijah, had predicted the birth of a son to the respectable Sunammite woman who had given hospitality to him and his servant. When the child grew into a boy and suddenly died, Elisha resuscitated him with the warmth of his body (2 Kings, 4, 32–37), just as Elijah had done with the son of the widow of Sarephta. In the painting we see the boy in his mother's arms, lying with his head hanging down, apparently still dead. It is not clear which is the precise moment depicted, whether the commanding gesture of the prophet's right hand is addressed to the woman or whether it is intended to revive the boy. Januarius Zick was, like his father Johann, both architect and painter and, also like his father, he produced his most valuable creations in the sphere of mural painting. His Rembrandtesque manner, once more like his father's, is restricted to small-size panels and canvases like this one.

Lower right
JANUARIUS ZICK
(JOHANN RASSO JANUARIUS ZICKH)
Munich 1730—Ehrenbreitstein 1797
Elisha and the Sunammite Boy
Oil on walnut panel, 40.3 × 27.6 cms.
Inv. no. 6671.
Formerly in the collection of Count Beleznay,
Budapest. Donated to the Museum in 1933 by
Rudolf Bedö.

ANGELICA KAUFMANN. *Portrait of a Woman.* p. 139

The young woman in her fashionable, playful disguise represents "Venus at her dressing-table." If it is true that this artificial picture portrays the widowed Princess Esterházy, *née* Galicin, we could—not without malice and aforethought—remark that it is a case of a widow painting a widow; for Angelica, divorced from her deceiving first husband, had just that year lost her second spouse, the painter Antonio Zacchi. The painting is certainly no self-portrait, as had been thought for a long time, and the dancelike posture is imitated to a considerable degree from the Farnese *Aphrodite Kallipygos* (Museo Nazionale, Naples)—a Hellenistic statue preserved in a Roman copy, which Angelica and her contemporaries frequently used as a model for their paintings. Together with the Venetian paintress Rosalba Carriera and the Frenchwoman Elisabeth Vigée-Lebrun, our Swiss lady artist belongs to the generation that links Rococo with Neo-Classicism, and all three experienced real artistic and social triumphs in their time. Among Angelica's numerous genius friends were Winckelmann, Reynolds, Herder, and Goethe, all of whom were portrayed by her. Winckelmann introduced her to Classical Antiquity, Reynolds contemplated marrying her, and Herder called her "perhaps the most cultivated woman in Europe." Goethe, to whom she was "my best Roman acquaintance," was, to be sure, not quite satisfied with her portrait of him. In 1787, while she was still portraying him, he wrote that there was quite a nice boy in the picture, but no trace of his own self.

ANGELICA KAUFFMANN
Chur (Graubünden) 1741—Rome 1807
Portrait of a Woman
Oil on cloth, 131 × 103 cms.;
Signed and dated at lower left (beneath the pillar):
Angelica Kauffmann Pinx: Romae a⁰ 1795.
Inv. no. 444.
From the Esterházy Collection. A preliminary chalk design is preserved at the Vorarlberger Landemuseum, Bregenz.

WILHELM LEIBL. *Portrait of Pál Szinyei Merse.* p. 140

The origins of this painting are well-known through the writings of the critic Julius Meier-Graefe and other sources. The portrait is not only an excellent example of Leibl's early painting, but also a first-rate historical document in itself. The immense impression on certain young Munich painters made by seven Courbet canvases exhibited in 1869 at the international exhibition in a special room of the Glass Palace, was heightened by Leibl's personal encounter with Courbet, who arrived in Munich on the first of October that year. Exactly one month later, the twenty-five-year-old Leibl (who was known to have spent months painting a single detail in his inordinately meticulous style) dashed off "in one brush-stroke, just like Courbet," this portrait of his young Hungarian friend. The date is unmistakably recorded in their reminiscences, for it was both Leibl's and Szinyei Merse's last day at the school of Karl Piloty, a celebrated history painter, then the top authority at the Munich Academy. The very next day the two young men left Piloty's school in protest. The portrait remained unfinished, for Leibl had accepted Courbet's invitation to go to Paris, where he remained until the outbreak of the Franco-Prussion War. Both Leibl and his model have assured themselves a significant place in the history of art. A fanatic of unadorned truth, Leibl has risen to the forefront of 19th-century German realism.

JAN KUPECKÝ. *Self-Portrait with Wife and Son.*
This free-thinking and eccentric, somewhat conservative but genuinely honest painter, whose birthplace is unknown, has been claimed by several nations. His parents, members of the persecuted religious sect of Bohemian Brothers, had to withdraw to Slovakia, and the artist remained faithful to their persuasion, and he had to move from place to place.

Here the artist's family is depicted unembellished, in its genre-like everyday surrounding, in dark, heavy colors and pronounced *chiaroscuro*. The little son, aged two or three, and the artist, bearing more than fifty years on his shoulders, both establish contact with the viewer through their eyes. According to the scheme and patriarchal tradition, they should therefore represent the "active" part of the family. But the appearance is deceptive. Although the artist's wife is "passively" staring at some point in front of her, she is the one who dominates the composition. She is the tallest and the most brightly lit, and though by no means in the prime of her youth, her face irradiates energy.

Left
WILHELM LEIBL
Cologne 1844—Würzburg 1900
Portrait of Pál Szinyei Merse (1869)
Oil on canvas, 139.5 × 102 cms.
Inv. no. 10 B.
Donated to the Museum in 1900 by Pál Szinyei Merse.

Right and detail p. 142
JAN KUPECKÝ
Prague or Pezinok near Bratislava, 1667—Nuremberg 1740
Self-Portrait with Wife and Son (circa 1718–19)
Oil on canvas, 111 × 91 cms.
Inv. no. 3922.
The painting was in the artist's estate in Nuremberg. Later it hung in Ansbach Castle, then in the J. Porgès Collection, Paris. Donated to the Museum in 1910 by Marcell Nemes.

141

JAN KUPECKÝ
Self-Portrait with Wife and Son (circa 1718–19),
detail.

MARTIN VAN MEYTENS. *Self-Portrait.*   *p. 143*

Martin van Meytens (or Mytens) was, as his name indicates, of Dutch descent (his father was born in The Hague). His period of intense international activities was followed by almost four decades in Vienna, where he was busy as official portrait painter to the Habsburg-Lotharingian court, and from 1759 also as director of the Art Academy. Our self-portrait shows him in his function as court painter. He is depicted in a green suit and a lavish red velvet coat, with a powdered wig, cleanly shaven, corpulent and self-conscious. He wears a gold necklace with the medallion portrait of the Swedish king Frederick I (1720–1751), who had likewise wanted to retain him at his court, while his right hand is displaying a miniature portrait of the empress Maria Theresia (1740–1780). Quite apart from the self-contented presentation of the painter's high patrons and of the honors received, the hand holding the miniature of the empress itself represents a special branch of Baroque self-portraiture, i.e., "the painter showing off his works." In our case we must remember that Meytens had been, from his first beginnings in England, an appreciated and much sought-after miniaturist.

FRANZ ANTON MAULBERTSCH. *Rebecca and Eliezer at the Well.*   *p. 144*

Rebecca is offering a drink to Abraham's servant, whom his master had sent out to find a wife for his son Isaac. Illustrations of this biblical scene had been known since the 6th century, from the miniatures in the famous *Vienna Genesis.* Here we find it staged by the leading master not merely of Austrian, but of all Central European Baroque painting. Maulbertsch, to whom the critic Garas has definitively ascribed this painting, brilliantly fused the various influences from the contemporary Venetian colorists

MARTIN VAN MEYTENS
Stockholm 1695—Vienna 1770
Self-Portrait (1740–41)
Oil on canvas, 65 × 50.2 cms.
Inv. no. 2221.
Bought in 1902 from a private Hungarian owner.

(Piazzetta, Pittoni) and from the painters of South-German Rococo, and through them indirectly from Rembrandt. The ancient legend has here become pervaded by irreality and fantasy. The picturesque baroque well is bathed in a miraculous light, the two protagonists are elongated in Mannerist fashion, and Rebecca herself, with a precious pitcher that could hardly ever serve to fetch water from a well, resembles the elegantly coquettish figures from the *Commedia dell'arte*, revived at roughly the same time in porcelain by Bustelli. The mulberry bush (in German, *Maulbeerstrauch*), near the boys at left, serves as the painter's signature.

144

FRANZ ANTON MAULBERTSCH
(MAULPERTSCH)
Langenargen, on Lake Constance, 1724—
Vienna 1796
Rebecca and Eliezer at the Well
(circa 1755–60)
Oil on canvas, 73 × 90.5 cms.
Inv. no. 66.12.

FRANCE
ENGLAND

SIMON VOUET. *Apollo and the Muses.*

All the depictions of Mount Parnassus—from Raphael down to Mengs and Appiani—are centered on *Apollo Musagetes,* shown here with his lyre, and flanked by the Muses. Vouet, a virtuoso decorator, who does not bother to characterize his figures, has added a figure personifying the sacred Castalian Spring to the five Muses on the left, while the four Muses on the right are supplemented by the two putti placed near Urania's globe. This well-balanced composition is crowned by the evanescent figure of a prancing Pegasus, far away among the clouds and olive trees at upper left. The picture, created at some time in the 1630s, is a good example of Vouet's affably idealized world, in which all the contrasts are brilliantly harmonized. The artist sojourned fifteen years in Italy, where he at first modeled himself on Caravaggio, and then gradually drifted toward Reni's and Lanfranco's orbit. In 1624 he became *principe* of the Academy of St. Luke, Rome, and stayed on in the Apennine Peninsula until Louis XIII and Richelieu called him back to Paris. The year of his return—1627—marks for modern art historians the beginning of French "national" painting. In fact, his Paris workshop trained some of the artists who decisively influenced later developments in French painting, notably Le Sueur, Le Brun and Mignard, and the glorious garden-designer André Le Notre. In this particularly sunny period, the *Premier Peintre du Roi* lived at the Louvre, painted altarpieces and pastel portraits, and above all decorated numerous royal residences and private houses in Paris.

SIMON VOUET
Paris 1590—Paris 1649
Apollo and the Muses
Oil on fir panel, 80 × 221.5 cms.
Inv. no. 707.
From the Esterházy Collection.

CLAUDE LORRAIN. *Villa in the Roman Campagna.*   *p. 147*

Landscape as an independent subject first appeared in Northern European painting. In the south, namely in Italy, it developed out of the internationally connected Roman art of about 1600, headed by Annibale Carracci, Elsheimer and Bril. But the great creators of ideal landscape were unquestionably the two Frenchmen, Poussin and Claude Lorrain. Both worked almost all their lives in Rome, for a period almost as neighbors, and up to Poussin's death in excellent personal relations, although as artists diametri-

cal opposites. While Poussin, a classicist with a feeling for plastic form, can be linked to Carracci and other Bolognese painters—always laying stress on man, dramatizing and rationally ordering nature—Claude, in his picturesqueness a precursor of the Romantics, painted "pure" landscapes. In spite of his schooling (his teacher Agostino Tassi was a pupil of Bril), he had closer ties with the Northern painters: his human figures are reduced to mere accessories and strictly subordinated to emotionally experienced nature, and the main subject of his paintings emerges in the sensitive exploration of the changing light at various times of the day. Our painting, for instance, shows the shadows lengthening as the day verges into evening, how they are deepest among the trees and along the water, where the shepherd is seen returning with his flock, while the warm sunlight is still flooding the noble building in the background, the distant bay, the mountains behind it, and the sky. In this quiet, spacious, paradisiacal landscape remote from all evil, serving as a frame for a pastoral existence that has remained unchanged for centuries, we can recognize echoes from biblical and saintly legends, mythology and classical poetry, Vergil, Ovid and Tasso.

CLAUDE LORRAIN (CLAUDE GELLÉE)
Chamagne near Nancy 1600—Rome 1682
Villa in the Roman Campagna (circa 1640–46)
Oil on canvas, 68.8 × 91 cms.
Inv. no. 708.
From the Esterházy Collection. The *Liber Veritatis* lists our painting under no. 107. According to the same source the painter's client was Duke Pamphilius. A similar painting is in the Hermitage, Leningrad.

147

LAURENT DE LA HIRE. *Theseus and Aethra.*

The literary sources for this picture are found in Plutarch and in the *Fabulae* or *Genealogiae* of the Roman mythographer Hyginus. The young Greek hero Theseus, led by his mother Aethra, finds the sword and footwear of his father Aegeus under a rock. Laurent de La Hire—who was one of the fourteen founding members of the *Académie Royale* created in 1648—had never visited Italy. His feeling for the ideal world of classical beauty was inspired by Nicolas Poussin who had previously depicted the same subject during his Paris period (1640–42; Musée Condé, Chantilly). La Hire's painting lacks the firmness and austerity that distinguish Poussin's art. Everything is pleasant, mild and attractive—reflecting, as it were, the great masters of his time on a subdued scale. Against the golden-toned landscape setting, with the remains of an ancient column on a pedestal, all the color is concentrated on the foreground figures. Theseus, busy lifting a heavy stone block, is given prominence by lively touches of red to underline the young man's heroic character.

Lower left
LAURENT DE LA HIRE (LA HYRE)
Paris 1606—Paris 1656
Theseus and Aethra
Oil on canvas, 141 × 118.5 cms.
Inv. no. 693.
From the Esterházy Collection, like two other paintings by La Hire in the Museum (*Ninus Offering a Crown to Semiramis* and *The Virgin and Child*).

Below
JEAN-BAPTISTE SIMÉON CHARDIN
Paris 1699—Paris 1779
Still-Life with Hanging Turkey
Oil on canvas, 96 × 123 cms.
Signed at lower left on the stone slab: *Chardin*.
Inv. no. 8898.
In the Museum since 1948. Previously in the collection of Mór Lipó Herzog, Budapest, and before that in the collection of Marcell Nemes, Munich.

JEAN-BAPTISTE SIMÉON CHARDIN. *Still-Life with Hanging Turkey.*

In the context of 18th-century French painting, with its fashionable elegance, eroticism and later, the thundering moralist pathos of Neo-Classicism—which so irresistibly and powerfully dictated European taste—Chardin's work is a remarkable exception. This first real painter of reality since the Le Nain brothers belonged to the petty bourgeoisie, with simple down-to-earth habits. Restrained, sober, precise and thrifty, he painted

calmly and faithfully only what he actually saw and knew well. He neither aspired to quick virtuoso brush-strokes, nor to noble or seductive subjects. Applying almost unmixed colors, one against the other, without transitions, he prefigured Impressionism. If he was able, so to speak, to reproduce real objects in all their palpable corporeality, he always interlinked them with unprecedented harmonies of color tones, hues and reflections. His copper pots and glassware, which appear again and again in his pictures, become intimately familiar. We can even tell at what point, in spite of his slow method of painting and his relatively modest remuneration—which never quite matched that of the painters of fashionable portraits and large-sized histories—he was able to buy some precious porcelain or other object, which thenceforth regularly appears in his paintings. So he passed in isolation through the decades of frivolous and decorative Rococo; and toward the end of his life, when ill and with failing eyesight, he painted his marvelous pastels, he remained no less impervious to all the new things emerging.

HUBERT ROBERT
Paris 1733—Paris 1808
Ancient Ruins
Oil on cardboard, 32.8 × 24.8 cms.
Inv. no. 665.
From the Esterházy Collection. Earlier it had belonged to Josef Fischer, director of the Vienna Gallery.

HUBERT ROBERT. *Ancient Ruins.*

The monuments of periods long since vanished seem mightier than the insignificant trivial structures of the contemporary world. Though ruined, they still rise victoriously against the sky. Hubert Robert—who, as we happen to know, had been of cheerful disposition in real life—appears in his works a melancholy *laudator temporis acti.* He is evidently identifying with the two nameless figures lost in contemplation at the foot of a fallen obelisk. The Roman triumphal arch facing them had never appeared more magnificent, even though now neglected and its crumbling stone sprouting with greenery, and even though—what profanation!—at this very moment a peasant's ox-cart is creaking beneath it. This master of picturesquely rendered and romantically felt classical remains came to be called simply *Robert des ruines,* for his favorite subject matter. He was a real child of his time, rendering homage both to the Neo-Classicism that dominated contemporary Europe, and to the pre-Romanticism announcing the art of the 19th century.

CAMILLE COROT. *Woman with a Daisy.*   *p. 150*
Like Corot's numerous—and so often copied—silvery landscapes (cf. *Louvre/Paris,* page 106), his portraits of women quietly re-create a world of subtle color harmonies all his own: self-contained, intimate, and accordingly poetical. In his canvases, the humane, kind-hearted, but in no sense revolutionary artist revived something of the poetry he so deeply admired in the old masters, poets of tranquil existence, like Giorgione and other Venetians of the Renaissance period, or Vermeer in 17th-century Holland.

Facing page
CAMILLE COROT
Paris 1796—Paris 1875
Woman with a Daisy (circa 1870)
Oil on canvas, 78 × 58 cms.
Inv. no. 501 B.
In the Museum since 1946. Before that in the
collection of Mór Lipó Herzog, Budapest, and
prior to that in the Dollfuss Collection, Paris.

GUSTAVE COURBET
Ornans 1819—La Tour-de-Peilz 1877
The Wrestlers
Oil on canvas, 252 × 198 cms.
Signed at lower left, and dated 1853.
Inv. no. 502 B.
Auctioned in 1882 at the Hôtel Drouot, Paris.
Through the mediation of the Berlin art dealer
Bruno Cassirer the painting was acquired by the
Budapest collector Ferenc Hatvanyi. In the
Museum since 1951.

Our painting of a young woman not particularly outstanding for her beauty is typical of his late work, like his famous *Woman with a Pearl*, in the Louvre, patterned on Leonardo's *Mona Lisa*, the Hamburg *Woman with a Rose*, and the São Paulo *Gypsy with a Mandolin* (cf. Art Museum/São Paulo, page 57). The painter gave the painting, still unfinished, to his friend Gaspard Lacroix, thus deceivingly making him seem more daring and modern than he actually cared to be.

GUSTAVE COURBET. *The Wrestlers*.
At the 1853 Salon the essentially self-taught pioneer of realism exhibited three paintings: *Two Bathers, The Sleeping Spinstress,* and *The Wrestlers*. At this Salon only the *Spinstress* was shown mercy by the public and the critics. Napoleon III was so disgusted by the *Two Bathers* that he struck at

it with his riding whip, and both this and our present picture were criticized even by the artist's friends. It must be conceded that this picture of two wrestlers is not considered one of Courbet's supreme masterpieces even today. Above all we feel uneasy about its pronounced duality: in the foreground the two sculpture-like life-size male nudes, frozen in a momentary attitude; and far behind, without any connection with them, the pictorially rendered tribunes thronged with spectators, and the stagy trees. But it is the subject matter that assures to Courbet's *Wrestlers* their eminent place in art; for it is this picture that introduces sport as a subject for painting.

ÉDOUARD MANET
Paris 1832—Paris 1883
Lady with a Fan (1862)
Oil on canvas, 90 × 113 cms.
Signed at lower left.
Inv. no. 368 B.
Bought in Berlin in 1916. The preliminary design, in watercolor, is preserved at the Kunsthalle, Bremen.

EDOUARD MANET. *Lady with a Fan.*
The woman reposing on a couch, with her dress spread out and a half-open fan in her left hand, is Jeanne Duval, a Creole beauty born in San Domingo, whose liaison with Baudelaire created quite a scandal in the bourgeois, conservative Paris of the time. This canvas was painted the year the poet of the *Fleurs du mal* had left her and moved to Brussels. The author of the painting, Edouard Manet, though serving as a kind of "banner around which the Impressionists gathered," never actually belonged to Impressionism in the strict sense of the word; but he tore painting away from the traditional illusionism of three-dimensionality, and thus opened the floodgate for all later developments. The overall impression of his *Lady with a Fan* might have been called a "harmony in white and green," by Manet's and Baudelaire's common acquaintance, James McNeill Whistler. The painting dates from Manet's so-called "Spanish period," when he was attracted to Spanish subjects, and modeled himself on Velázquez and Goya.

PAUL CÉZANNE
Aix-en-Provence 1839—Aix-en-Provence 1906
Cupboard, 1873–77
Oil on canvas, 65 × 81 cms.
Inv. no. 371 B.
In the Museum since 1917. Previously in the collection of Marcell Nemes.

PAUL CÉZANNE. *Cupboard.* *p. 153*

No other 19th-century artist has so decisively influenced the painting of the first half of our century as Cézanne, here represented by a typical still-life from his so-called Impressionist period—a painting whose colors—blue, red, green, and the reddish-green of the wine bottles—are described in a letter written by Rainer Maria Rilke to his wife Clara a year after the painter's death. Today, thanks to Meyer Schapiro's well-known essay on Cézanne's apples, we see in the master's still-life not merely a sphere of painting ideally suited for his solutions of purely artistic problems ("how to turn Impressionism into something durable," as repeated in all the hand-

books), but also a disguised, more or less subconscious expression of the artist's private passions and sensibilities—a microcosm, in which this passionate, but shy man could unleash, in sublimated form, his erotic fantasies. Renoir recalled Cézanne's statement that he painted still-lifes because female models frightened him. In this sense can be explained the bulging forms of the apples—on a tablecloth which is crumpled like a white mountain—as a substitute for human bodies. . . .

PAUL GAUGUIN. *Two Black Hogs and a Horse.*   *p. 155*

In all periods artists have traveled, fled, and moved, both in actual life and in fancy—otherwise art could hardly exist. But few travels have borne such abundant fruit and impressed themselves so deeply on the history of European culture as Gauguin's flight from civilization. This eternal rebel against convention, who had already expressed all the essential traits of *fin de siècle* art in his famous *Vision after a Sermon* (1888, National Gallery of Scotland, Edinburgh), seemed predestined from birth to forge a link between European and non-European art. Stressed outlines (*cloisonnisme*) and compact, pure, almost unarticulated color surfaces (*synthétisme*) are already present in his Pont-Aven period. If he was able to discover on Tahiti an exuberantly bright-colored nature—the almost unreal "lost paradise" he had always searched for—we are well aware that it was because he carried all its intrinsic traits in his own self. In the florid beauty surrounding him, his restless spirit was able incessantly to commune with his own inner landscapes, remote both in time and space. Many of his masterpieces were inspired by some yellowed photograph he happened to have, perhaps a snapshot of a sculpture from Borobodur, or an 18th-Dynasty Egyptian painting. And if not in 1891, then certainly after finally settling in Polynesia, he came to realize that he could not escape European civilization even thousands of miles from his native country, and that even amidst his paradise he was destined to carry with him his own personal hell, increasingly unbearable as he approached his end. In the course of all these experiences he created masterpieces which revolutionized art—tender and melancholy works, marvelous and deeply moving elegies built up of vivid, pure colors.

CAMILLE PISSARRO. *Pont Neuf, Paris.*   *p. 156*

During the last ten years of his life the old Pissarro, whom an eye disease was increasingly hindering from open-air painting, continued to paint from hotel windows and garret rooms: Paris and Rouen, the quays of Le Havre and Dieppe, and again and again the avenues, boulevards, squares and bridges of Paris. Human beings had always been an important element in his canvases, and present in almost all of his landscapes, in contrast to those of the other French Impressionists. It is no mere accident or result of external circumstances that it was Pissarro who became the painter of the man-conceived, man-built and man-inspired stony landscapes of cities. At a time when the Impressionist vision was almost exhausted, these panoramic pictures of human ant hills once more bring to life all its splendor with

154

PAUL GAUGUIN
Paris 1848—Atuana (Marquesas Islands) 1903
Two Black Hogs and a Horse
Oil on canvas, 91 × 72 cms.
Signed and dated at lower right: *P. Gauguin 91.*
Inv. no. 355 B.
Bought in 1913 at the Gauguin exhibition, Budapest.

Facing page
CAMILLE PISSARRO
St. Thomas (Antilles) 1831—Paris 1903
Pont Neuf, Paris
Oil on canvas, 55 × 46.5 cms.
Signed at lower left and dated 1902.
Inv. no. 205 B.
Purchased in 1907.

HENRI DE TOULOUSE-LAUTREC
Albi 1864—Château de Malromé 1901
Ces Dames (1895)
Oil on cardboard, 60.3 × 80.5 cms.
Signed at lower left: *T. Lautrec.*
Inv. no. 356 B.
Bought in 1913 at the Toulouse-Lautrec
exhibition, Budapest.

thousands of shimmering reflections. In the tremulous silvery atmosphere of this canvas can be recognized the masses of people, carriages and other vehicles swarming to and fro over the oldest and most famous of the Seine bridges, so often depicted by painters and graphic artists from Callot to Marquet and our own time. The white-haired master, who painted the subject from a window high up on the Place Dauphine, had traveled a long way to these last creations. He was the oldest of the Impressionists, a venerated patriarch to all of them, and at the same time the only one whose heart was open to the younger generation and able to enrich itself along with them.

HENRI DE TOULOUSE-LAUTREC. *Ces Dames.*
The crippled, dwarfish aristocrat Toulouse-Lautrec, a genius and one of the early-to-die *peintres maudits*, has left us a disarmingly frank image of end-of-the-century bohemian Paris, to which he himself belonged in all of his activities. It is through his eyes that we are still able to discover the glamour

and the everyday reality of Paris' *belle époque*: the cabarets and dancing establishments, circuses and brothels, the artists and performers, some of them still famous, others forgotten even during their lifetime, the "stars," the prostitutes and the *bon vivants*. Everywhere—in his paintings, his lithographs or his famous lithographed posters—his attention was centered on people; everywhere he captures, with an unusually quick and assured stroke, the movements, postures and facial expressions, instinctively avoiding anything redundant to characterization. He simply evaded the problems of lighting, which incessantly engaged the Impressionists, as if they did not exist. In our painting the most ordinary scene is brought to life with sparse outlines and bright colors, which, as usual in his works, barely cover the painted surface, thus contributing to the overall effect. We see a few pinkish, fleshy, faded and bored female inhabitants of the so-called *maisons closes*, whom certainly no other artist, earlier or later, has known more intimately and portrayed more truthfully.

SIR JOSHUA REYNOLDS
Plympton (Plymouth) 1723—London 1792
Portrait of Admiral Sir Edward Hughes
(1786–87)
Oil on canvas, 76 × 63 cms.
Inv. no. 458.
From the Esterházy Collection. According to
Reynolds' notebook, the painting was acquired
in 1787 by Duke Esterházy, then ambassador of
the Viennese Imperial Court.

SIR JOSHUA REYNOLDS. *Portrait of Admiral Sir Edward Hughes.*   *p. 159*
Reynolds—first president of the *Royal Academy*, founded in 1768—endeavored to raise portrait-painting to the level of historical painting, which at that time was much more highly appreciated. Therefore he often carried out his single, double and group portraits in playful mythological or historical disguise. His models often show quite unportrait-like activities. In addition to genre-like scenes of reading or profound thinking in the sense of *Et in Arcadia ego*, there are plenty of other possibilities: mothers playing with their children, young men at their archery exercises, an actor hesitating between Comedy and Tragedy, young noblewomen as Ste. Geneviève or as the Three Graces decorating the statue of Hymen, and even children forced to appear in the disguise of Henry VIII or St. George. The scope of his pictures varies vastly, from full-length figures that certainly seem best suited for such a masquerade, to more modest dimensions like those of our painting, which presents a contented, red-cheeked admiral. The picture belongs to the late period of the great eclectic, who gave to his compatriots a veritable synthesis of representative European portrait painting; but in the decade after his stay in Flanders, to which this canvas belongs, he once again became somewhat more natural and immediate, though his protagonists still tend to look the way the inhabitants of Albion have always wanted to be portrayed: either important or intelligent or both.

158

159

JOHN CONSTABLE. *Celebration of the Battle of Waterloo at East Bergholt.*

When contemplating this uncommonly picturesque and free presentation of
the artist's native town—the crowd rejoicing around a huge puppet image
of Napoleon hanging from the gallows, the trees and flags and clouds—we
must not forget that this fresh, vivid little spontaneous painting was only
the preliminary color design for a much less unrestrained and much more
conventional "finished" picture, which in this case was never realized. But
even accepting this reservation, the little canvas strikingly proves the quite
exceptional "progressiveness" of Constable's landscape-painting, which was
first discovered on the Continent in the 1820s, especially at the 1824 Paris
Salon, when his famous *Hay-Cart* of 1821 was exhibited together with his
View of the Stour at Dedham, painted one year later. After exerting a
decisive influence upon Delacroix at the time, his creations later influenced
the Barbizon painters and—at least indirectly—the Impressionists. His
compatriots, however, only recognized Constable's importance as the foremost landscape painter after the 17th-century masters through the mediation of France, and in particular from the moment when his formerly
unknown oil sketches for the first time left his studio to be shown, in 1888,
as a legacy of his daughter, at the Victoria and Albert Museum (then called
South Kensington Museum), London.

160

JOHN CONSTABLE
East Bergholt (Suffolk) 1776—London 1837
*Celebration of the Battle of Waterloo
at East Bergholt*
Oil on canvas, 23 × 33.5 cms.
Inv. no. 4624.
Bought in 1913 from Dr. Herman Eissler,
Vienna. Earlier in the collection P. A. Chéramy,
Paris, and before that it had belonged to the art
dealers Charles Sedelmeyer, Paris, and
Th. Agnew, London.

HISTORY OF THE MUSEUM
AND PLAN OF THE BUILDING

The origins of the art collections in the Museum of Fine Arts are rooted in the distant past, although the art legacy of the Hungarian rulers was for the most part destroyed in the wars and devastation of the 16th and 17th centuries. The process of assembling and conserving art treasures was interrupted by the Turkish incursions, the fall of Buda, and the division of the country into three parts, which resulted in the transfer of many precious imperial possessions to Vienna and Prague. It was only after the expulsion of the Turks and the country's liberation in the 18th century that a cultural revival occurred, prompting the systematic collection of art treasures.

The first public collection in Hungary was started during a perod of rising national consciousness. In 1802 Count Ferenc Széchényi founded the National Museum, with the aim of assembling and preserving mementoes of Hungary's past. But between 1832 and 1836 the scope of the Museum's collections was widened through the acquisition of a large group of medieval and Italian art objects belonging to Miklós Janković of Pest, and almost immediately came the legacy of János Lászlo Pyrker, Archbishop of Eger, in 1836, which established the museum on a solid foundation. This latter important bequest consisted of 192 valuable art treasures, most of them purchased by the archbishop early in the century when he was patriarch in Venice. Through it the Museum acquired such outstanding Italian Renaissance paintings as Gentile Bellini's *Portrait of Catherine Cornaro*, Giorgione's *Portrait of a Young Man*, Paolo Veronese's *Allegory of Venice*, Memling's *Triptych with the Crucifixion* and Tiepolo's *Madonna with Six Saints.*

In 1848, during the Hungarian War of Independence, the National Museum was further enriched by yet another group of important pictures. By order of the liberal leader Lajos Kossuth, 78 paintings were transferred from his apartment in Buda, and thus came into public ownership. Before coming to the royal palace in Buda, these paintings had been taken in the 18th century from the Vienna imperial collection to the Pozsony Palace in Bratislava, then the capital of Hungary. They were mostly small in dimension, but extremely valuable works, the majority dating from the 17th century, formerly in the well-known Brussels and Vienna galleries of the archduke Leopold William, the majority traceable to 17th-century English and Venetian collections. The most remarkable of these paintings, now all in the Museum of Fine Arts, are Dürer's *Portrait of a Man*, Palma Vecchio's beautiful *Young Couple*, Lorenzo Lotto's *Sleeping Apollo and the Muses*, several Tintoretto portraits and a few notable works by Lucas Cranach the Elder.

In the 1860s another exceptional collection could be seen in Pest. This was the Esterházy gallery which had been moved from Vienna. Belonging to Hungary's most distinguished aristocratic family, this extraordinary collection was assembled for the most part toward the end of the 18th and beginning of the 19th century by Prince Miklós Fényes (1714–1799) and his grandson Prince Miklós II (1765-1833). During and after the French Revolution and Napoleonic wars, when a great many works of art were changing hands, the Esterházys took advantage of these circumstances by buying paintings and drawings of inestimable value in Italy, France and Austria. Then in 1819 and 1821 Prince Miklós for the first time started

162

acquiring Spanish paintings through the Danish ambassador in Spain, thus laying the foundation of the uniquely valuable collection of Spanish paintings, which is today one of the major attractions of the Museum. In 1820 Prince Miklós purchased at auction the collection of the Habsburg statesman Wenzel Anton von Kaunitz, thus acquiring such notable works as Ribera's *Martyrdom of St. Andrew*, Goya's *Water-Carrier* and *Knife-Grinder*, as well as Rubens' and van Dyck's *Mucius Scaevola in the Presence of Porsenna.*

For a long time the Esterházy collection had been scattered in the various family palaces, but in 1814 all the works were assembled at Mariahilf, the Esterházy palace in Vienna, and the collection became a city attraction. Open to the public three days a week, the gallery was described by reviewers and travelers of the period, and it was through a catalogue published in 1812 that the most outstanding of these works entered the pages of art history.

By 1860 the amount of attention engendered by the Esterházy collection aroused the general feeling that the collection should be moved to Budapest, and help to compensate for the art treasures lost in previous centuries. Complying with this wish, Prince Pál Esterházy in 1865 transferred the collection to Pest and it was temporarily accommodated in the newly-built palace of the Hungarian Academy of Science. Toward the end of 1870 the Esterházy family encountered financial difficulties and offered the collection for sale. It was immediately purchased by the Hungarian government, and the sum of 1,100,000 gold forints was paid for its 635 paintings of inestimable value. In 1871 the collection became the State Gallery, forerunner of the future great state Museum of Art.

The paintings which came from the Esterházy family, first accommodated in the State Gallery and then in the Museum of Fine Arts, are still recognized as the most valuable portion of Hungary's art treasures. They included such major Italian masterpieces as Raphael's *Madonna with the Infant Jesus and John the Baptist*—known as The Esterházy Madonna—and his *Portrait of a Young Humanist*, Correggio's *Madonna del Latte*, Veronese's *Way of the Cross*, and a large altarpiece by Tiepolo, *St. James the Greater.* There were numerous German and Dutch paintings in the collection. In addition to exceptional works by Rubens, van Dyck, Jordaens, Rembrandt and Frans Hals there was a whole series of fine 17th-century Flemish and Dutch landscapes, genre paintings and portraits. Of the numerically more restricted French representation, the most interesting were *Villa in the Roman Campagna* by Claude Lorrain and Simon Vouet's *Apollo and the Muses.* By far the most important part of the collection, however, were the Spanish paintings. With three Murillos—including his famous *Christ Distributing Bread to the Pilgrims*—along with canvases by Zurbarán, Alonso Cano and the two Goyas, *The Water-Carrier* and *The Knife-Grinder*, the Esterházy collection was even at that time considered an outstanding repository of Spanish painting.

The transfer of this priceless collection to Budapest gave great impetus to the further development of museums in Hungary. In 1872 the State Gallery acquired yet another outstanding group of paintings through the gift of 64 Italian primitives from Bishop Arnold Ipolyi, a pioneer in Hungarian art history and research. Most of these paintings were

163

assembled by J. A. Ramboux, an artist from Cologne, whose collection came up for auction in 1869. Ramboux was one of the first, early in the 19th century, to recognize the value of the Italian Trecento and Quattrocento panel paintings. Outstanding items in this collection include Giovanni Sassetta's *St. Thomas Aquinas Praying before the Altar of the Virgin*, and notable works by Spinello Aretino, Ambrogio Lorenzetti, Giovanni di Paolo, Sano di Pietro.

Toward the end of the 19th century the State Gallery, which by that time had already incorporated the National Museum paintings, expanded its holdings mainly through purchases. Károly Pulszky, then the director, made systematic and regular acquisitions, buying works from art dealers in Milan, Florence and Paris. In this manner a number of outstanding works arrived in Budapest: Barend van Orley's *Portrait of Charles V*, Rembrandt's *Dream of St. Joseph*, the *Portrait of a Man* formerly attributed to Raphael but now confirmed as the work of Sebastiano del Piombo, as well as numerous Italian Renaissance and Dutch 17th-century masterpieces. Notable also among the works acquired by Pulszky is a series of North Italian frescoes, detached from their original walls and transferred to canvas. These retain an important place among the exhibits of the Museum of Fine Arts. Pulszky also laid the foundations for what was to develop into a very fine collection of European sculpture.

As the collections grew, the State Gallery no longer had the space to accommodate all these new acquisitions, and larger, more suitable premises were needed to house those treasures. When the National Assembly convened in 1896 to commemorate the centenary of the birth of the nation, it was decided to build a new museum adequate in size for all its holdings. The architects Fülöp Herzog and Albert Schickendanz were engaged and in ten years' time the vast complex—covering more than 110,000 square feet—was completed, with its grandiose Neoclassic façade displaying a replica of the pediment sculpture group on the Temple of Zeus at Mt. Olympus. In deference to contemporary taste, plaster copies of classical, medieval, Renaissance and Baroque sculptures were displayed in the vast hall on the ground floor. The first floor hall was planned as the paintings gallery, and a special room was reserved for the collection of drawings and prints. The museum facilities were the most advanced of the time, and when the new building opened as the Museum of Fine Arts in 1906 it was recognized as one of the finest art museum buildings in Europe. In the years to come new acquisitions were made, and various legacies and purchases added to the collections. In 1912 came the legacy of Count János Pálffy, through which 121 paintings were added to the "Old Masters Gallery," while the Modern Gallery, devoted to the 19th century, acquired 56 works. From the János Pálffy collection came Titian's *Doge Marcantonio Trevisani*, Boltraffio's *Virgin and Child*, an unusually fine *Portrait of a Nobleman* by Veronese, the Petrus Christus *Virgin and Child* and numerous paintings of 17th-century Dutch masters. In 1908 and 1913 through the acquisition of the ancient art assembled by the German classical archaeologist Paul Arndt, the Museum's collection of Greek vases and sculptures was set on a firm foundation. Another important contribution was the legacy of István Ferenczy, a notable Hungarian sculptor whose collection assembled in Rome early in the 19th century contained priceless works. Among them was Leonardo da Vinci's famous equestrian bronze.

164   The First World War and the difficult aftermath slowed the development of the Museum: yet

new purchases, primarily of modern works, and the support of several patrons yielded further results. Mention should be made of the bequest of the Hungarian collector Marcell Nemes from Munich. This was the source of an outstanding El Greco, the *Repentant Magdalen,* as well as the *Portrait of Ferenc Rákóczi II* by Ádám Mányoki, which is now in the National Gallery. In the 1930s, thanks to the legacy of Pál Majovszky, the print collection acquired some extraordinarily beautiful 19th-century drawings, including a marvelous Delacroix water-color *Horse Frightened by Lightning,* and superb sheets by Manet, Degas, Renoir, Cézanne, Toulouse-Lautrec and others. During this period the Museum also acquired Manet's lovely canvas of his Spanish period, *Lady with a Fan* depicting Baudelaire's mistress, a Monet landscape and works by Puvis de Chavannes, Pierre Bonnard and others.

The Museum was severely damaged in the Second World War. A bomb fell on the building, the glass roof construction was completely demolished, and in the final period of the war the most important art treasures were assembled and hastily transported to Germany. These works were returned after the war, but many valuable pictures, particularly those of small dimensions, were lost forever.

Following the restoration of the building and its treasures in the 1940s, the Museum resumed normal activity, and the acquisition of several rich collections spurred on its further development. In 1951, the addition of the Ráth Museum in Budapest—which had previously been considered a separate foundation containing exceptional works assembled by György Ráth in the last century—brought to the Museum of Fine Arts a large number of important works, including Sebastiano del Piombo's *Portrait of a Girl,* Rembrandt's *Slaughtered Ox,* and other works. When the Hungarian capital acquired the Zichy Gallery through the legacy of Ödön and Jenö Zichy, the holdings of German and Austrian paintings were notably expanded. In addition to these large collections and the transfer of many works that had been kept in other museums but belonged thematically to the Museum of Fine Arts—for example classical sculpture—regular purchases also contributed to the rapid, planned development of the museum as a whole. Purchases of ancient Egyptian art and acquisitions resulting from Hungarian excavations in Nubia expanded the collections in this field, while in classical art, the holdings of vases and sculptures were significantly augmented.

The new acquisitions of paintings, often serving to fill in certain gaps, completed the already outstanding collections of the Old Masters Gallery. Notable works by Sebastiano Ricci, Tiepolo, the Guardi brothers and B. Bellotto provide a survey of the Venetian Settecento, and the painting *Sodom* by Girolamo Romanino helped to round out the representation of Italian Renaissance paintings. Additions were made to the 17th- and 18-century German and Austrian holdings, and the French collection was supplemented with works by Poussin and Chardin, as well as a few works from earlier periods, while to the outstanding Spanish collection were added another El Greco painting, a Zurbarán, and several other canvases. The last dozen years have brought considerable changes in the presentation of modern painting and sculpture. Through purchase, exchange and bequest, in addition to the support of outstanding Hungarian artists living abroad, a completely new collection has been produced, with outlines suggesting the latest trends in the development of art.

PLAN OF THE BUILDING

GROUND FLOOR

1 Office
1a Office
2 Reading Room
3 Library
4 Michelangelo Room
5 Print Collection
6 Office
7 Print Collection
8 Romanesque Court
9 Baroque Court and 19th-century
   European Sculpture
10 Renaissance Court
11 20th-century Art
12 Egyptian Antiquities
13 Staircase
13a Staircase
14 Greek and Roman Antiquities
15 Ionic Temple
16 Doric Temple
17 Classical Sculpture
18 Vestibule
19 Classical Art
20 Classical Sculpture
21 Doric Temple

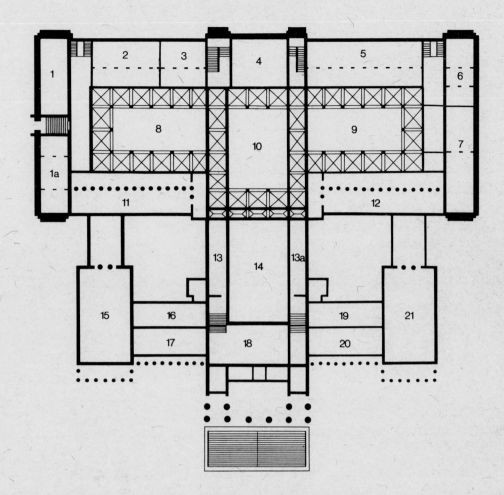

FIRST FLOOR

1 Modern Paintings Storage
2 Offices
3 Restoration Department
4 Exhibition Gallery
5 Old-Master Paintings Storage
6 English and French Painting
7 Flemish and Dutch Painting
8 German and Austrian Painting
9 Open space above the Romanesque Court
10 Renaissance Art around Open Space
   above Renaissance Court
11 Open Space above the Baroque Court
12 Offices
13 Flemish and Dutch Painting
14 Italian Painting
15 Spanish Painting
16 Italian Painting
17 Staircase
18 Hall
19 Staircase
20 Vestibule

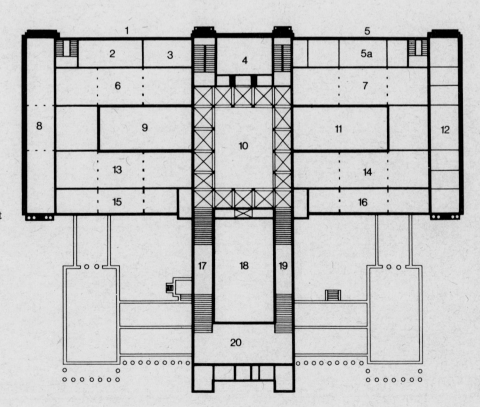

167

SELECTED BIBLIOGRAPHY

BOSKOVITS, MIKLÓS. *Early Italian Panel Paintings* (in the Budapest Museum of Fine Arts). Corvina Press, Budapest, 1966.

BUDAPEST MUSEUM OF FINE ARTS. *Catalogue of Paintings by Old Masters*, by Gabriel de Térey. Budapest, 1931.

CZOBOR, AGNES, EDITOR. *The Budapest Museum of Fine Arts.* Texts written by the research workers of the Budapest Museum of Fine Arts. Corvina Press, Budapest, 1970.

————*Dutch Landscapes in the Budapest Museum of Fine Arts.* Corvina, Budapest, 1967.

GARAS, KLÁRA. *The Budapest Gallery, Paintings in the Museum of Fine Arts.* Translated from the Hungarian. Corvina Press, Budapest, 1973.

GARAS, KLÁRA. *Italian Renaissance Portraits.* Corvina Press, Budapest, 1965.

GARAS, KLÁRA. *Poklady světového malířství v Budapešti: Obrazy z muzea výtvarných umění.* Odeon, Praha, 1975.

HARASZTI-TAKAS, MARIANNE. *Spanish Masters, Budapest Museum of Fine Arts.* Corvina Press, Budapest, 1966.

————*The Treasures of the Hungarian Museum of Fine Arts.* Corvina Press, Budapest, 1954.

MOJZER, MIKLOS. *Dutch Genre Paintings in the Budapest Museum of Fine Arts.* Corvina Press, Budapest, 1967

MRAVIK, LASZLO. *North Italian Fifteenth-Century Paintings* (Budapest Museum of Fine Arts). Corvina Press, Budapest, 1978.

PIGLER, ANDOR. *Museum der Bildenden Künste, Budapest: Katalog der alten Meister, I-II.* Akadémiai Kiadó, Budapest. 1957.

TEREY, GABRIEL VON. *Die Gemäldegalerie den Museums fur Bildende Künste in Budapest, I.* Julius Bard, Berlin, 1916.

————*Zeichnungen von Rembrandt Harmensz van Rijn in Budapester museum der bildende Künste.* Leipzig, 1909.

URBACH, SUSAN. *Early Netherlandish Painting in the Budapest Museum of Fine Arts.* Corvina Press, Budapest, 1971.

VAYER, L. *Master Drawings from the Collections of the Budapest Museum of Fine Arts.* Corvina Press, Budapest, (c. 1956).

VEGH, JÁNOS. *15th-Century German and Bohemian panel paintings in the Budapest Museum of Fine Arts.* Corvina Press, 1967.

————*16th-Century German Panel Paintings in the Budapest Museum of Fine Arts.* Corvina Press, Budapest, 1972.

ACTA HISTORIAE ARTIUM ACADEMIAE SCIENTIARUM HUNGARICAE. Budapest, izhaja.

BULLETIN DU MUSÉE HONGROIS DES BEAUX-ARTS. Budapest, izhaja.

PICTURE CREDITS

INDEX OF ILLUSTRATIONS

INDEX OF NAMES

GENERAL INDEX